"The Gift of Dhamma Excels All Other Gifts"

— The Lord Buddha

Mae Chee Kaew

Her Journey to Spiritual
Awakening and Enlightenment

Compiled from Thai sources & written by

Bhikkhu Dick Sīlaratano

A Forest Dhamma Publication

Mae Chee Kaew

A Forest Dhamma Publication / April 2009

Cover and interior design by Melita Halim.
Set in Centaur MT Std and Present LT Std.

ISBN 978-611-90205-0-4
Printed in Thailand by:
Silpa Siam Packaging and Printing Co., Ltd.
silpa@ksc.th.com
Tel. (662) 444-3351-9

Published by:
Forest Dhamma Books
Baan Taad Forest Monastery
Udon Thani 41000, Thailand
fdbooks@hotmail.com • fdbooks@gmail.com
www.ForestDhammaBooks.com

Contents

Part Three — Essence

Part Four — Purity

Mae Chee Kaew (1901 – 1991)

Preface

While I was living at Nakamnoi Forest Monastery in 2007, the abbot, Ajaan Intawai Santussako, asked me to translate a biographical sketch of Mae Chee Kaew from Thai into English, which he intended to publish in both languages. Although the sketch he gave me was rather brief, Ajaan Intawai graciously made available all previous writings about Mae Chee Kaew's life that he had collected. After translating the shortened version of her life into English, I decided to write a complete account based on more extensive research into the events that shaped her life and marked each step on her path to enlightenment. Nakamnoi Forest Monastery provided me with a calm and supportive environment in which to work, and the monks there provided valuable research assistance. Mae Chee Kaew's collected teachings, excerpts of which are quoted at the beginning of each chapter, presented a special challenge as most of them were recorded in her native Phu Tai dialect. I am indebted to those ethnic Phu Tai monks who helped me to decipher their meaning.

This book would not have been completed without the dedicated effort of many friends and helpers. My gratitude to them is immense. In particular, I would like to thank my longtime copyeditor, Swe Thant, for deftly smoothing over the rough edges of the first draft and helping to set the general tone of the narrative. Rachel Claveau then did a masterful job of trimming down superfluous language and improving the grammatical structure. Rachel also urged me to clarify many unclear or difficult passages to establish precisely the intended meaning. Special thanks go to Mae Chee Melita Halim, who single-handedly created the book's front and back cover designs, the interior design and all of the pencil drawings. She worked tirelessly for many months in difficult circumstances to prepare the manuscript for publication. I feel blessed to have a generous and enthusiastic publisher, Silpa Siam Packaging and Printing Co., Ltd., who not only facilitated the publication, but also helped to solicit contributions to fund the cost of printing. Without the generosity of many dedicated donors, it would not have been possible to print this book and make it available for free distribution. Their names are too numerous to mention, but each one of them deserves our heartfelt appreciation. And finally, a hearty thank you to Forest Dhamma Books, a worldwide network of friends, for the time and effort they volunteered in support of this project.

"When I went to the monastery as a young girl, I had to be accompanied by my parents, and I wasn't allowed to mingle with the monks. While listening to the monks discuss Dhamma, I sat way in the back, just within earshot. The venerable meditation master taught us how to pay homage to the Buddha and how to praise his virtues with chanting. He encouraged us to radiate loving kindness to all living beings, and to always be open-hearted and generous. He told us that no matter how generous we were as lay supporters, the virtue of that generosity could not compare with the virtue of ordaining as a white-robed nun and earnestly practicing the way to end all suffering. That message always remained close to my heart."

— Mae Chee Kaew

Introduction

*T*his book presents the life and the practice of a woman who reached the pinnacle of Buddhist practice in her lifetime. She was known as Mae Chee Kaew. Mae Chee Kaew felt the calling to a spiritual life at an early age. Blessed as a girl with the good fortune to meet some of the most renowned meditation masters of her era, she took their teachings on meditation to heart and, with youthful enthusiasm, earnestly put them into practice. Due to a favorable disposition, she soon developed into a child prodigy, skilled in the art of samādhi meditation. Her mind easily became absorbed in deep concentration for many hours, and was witness to many strange and wonderful occurrences.

When familial circumstances intervened to prevent her from undertaking a religious vocation, she bided her time patiently, waiting to take advantage of the earliest opportunity. After twenty years of unsatisfactory marriage, a door finally opened for Mae Chee Kaew and she stepped through, entering a life of renunciation. As a nun, she spent many years living and practicing with teachers of great renown. They often praised her for her extraordinary skills in meditation, especially her adeptness with psychic phenomena. Very few of them could equal her prowess in that field of perception. More significantly, however, she succeeded in overcoming her attachment to the conventional world with its ever-changing conditions, and thus attained the unconditioned state of total freedom. Being one of the few known female arahants of the modern era, she became living testimony that the Buddha's goal of supreme enlightenment is possible for everyone, regardless of gender, race or class.

Countless female practitioners lived during the time of the Buddha; most attained the fruits of the noble path, and many were praised by the Buddha. Over and over again in the Buddha's early discourses his female disciples were commended: they were lauded for their diligence, their wisdom and their teaching skills. There is no doubt that many women of that time left their families behind and devoted themselves to living the homeless life of a renunciant. In fact, when the Buddha started an order of nuns, many women rushed to join it. Due to the social constraints those women faced, that was an extraordinary achievement.

A man's willingness to turn his back on parents, spouse and children was viewed as evidence of his determination to seek the truth. It was considered virtuous for men to leave home and family behind for the sake of a spiritual vocation. Women, however, tread an altogether more difficult path to a life of renunciation. Enjoying far less freedom than men, they could not leave their families without first begging permission from reluctant spouses, and they were often constrained by duty to aging parents or young children. By starting an order of nuns, the Buddha was opening to women a unique opportunity to lead the homeless life in a way that transcended customary social and cultural constraints. He was also acknowledging that women are as capable of understanding the Dhamma as men, which was quite a radical notion at the time.

The Bhikkhunī Sangha was the community of nuns founded by the Buddha. It remained a thriving monastic order for over a millennium, but eventually the bhikkhunī linage died out due to war and famine. Because no mechanism for its revival was provided by the Buddha, the only ordination opportunity left open to women in Theravādan countries today is ordination as a nun, observing either eight or ten precepts. In Thailand, eight-precept nuns are the norm. They are known as *mae chees*. Like the monks, a *mae chee* shaves her head and undertakes training rules not generally observed by Buddhist lay people. Wearing distinctive white robes that reflect the strict division between the lifestyle of an ordained person and that of a layperson, a *mae chee* observes a standard code of discipline governing suitable attire, conduct and livelihood. She is not allowed to hire herself out, accept payment for jobs, or engage in the buying and selling of goods and services. She is instructed to keep in mind that a dignified appearance and exemplary behavior can encourage in others a genuine interest in the virtues of Buddhist practice.

Most *mae chees* reside in monasteries administered by monks. Smaller numbers live in their own nunneries, which are often associated with a local monastery. The practice-oriented monasteries, especially those in the Thai forest tradition, give women the free time and the basic requisites they need to pursue a lifestyle of renunciation and meditation. For this reason, many women prefer the opportunities for practice offered in *mae chee* communities affiliated with such monasteries. One perceived drawback to that arrangement is that the nuns are relegated to a status clearly secondary to that of the monks. This limitation is alleviated to some extent by the Buddhist understanding that authority and rank in a community are essentially social conventions needed to keep the community functioning smoothly. A woman's position in the hierarchy does not in any way reflect her essential worth as a person.

The separation of men and women has become so deeply ingrained in most cultures that it is quite natural to experience it in a religious context. But gender is transient, it comes and goes; conditioned by past karma, it is a kind of destiny. The essence of one's being is without name and without form, and thus without characteristics of male or female. This is a fundamental tenet of Buddhism: that the attributes of self-identity are devoid of intrinsic essence — everything that makes a person unique changes continually and eventually disintegrates. Each personality is constantly ceasing to be what it was and becoming something new. Those factors one tends to conceive of as "self" are impermanent and fleeting. Everything about bodily form, and the mind's thoughts and feelings, is without intrinsic worth and bound to dissolve. For that reason, clinging to body and mind is a major source of pain and suffering.

Realization that the essence of mind, stripped of all external characteristics, has no inherent gender, rank or status, liberates us from the concepts of separate or common identities that hinder our progress and limit our freedom. All such conventional distinctions must be transcended if we are to sever the bonds that bind us so tightly to the cycle of birth and death. In this respect, all human beings stand on an equal footing, because the fundamental delusions of mind that must be overcome are essentially the same for everyone.

Nothing is more amazing than the mind — it is extraordinary what a well-trained mind can do. By nature, Mae Chee Kaew's mind tended to be bold and dynamic. Prophetic dreams and psychic visions occurred effortlessly in her meditation. Her psychic tendencies were both a liability and a source of strength. For years their attraction blinded her to the need for self-restraint. Later, when she learned how to discipline her mind she was able to use her unusual abilities in profound and wondrous ways.

But inherent tendencies of mind vary significantly from one person to another. Some, like Mae Chee Kaew, are quite active and venturesome; others are more reserved and cautious. Each has its advantages in meditation. Mae Chee Kaew's dynamic mind allowed her to progress quickly along a path of practice that most people find to be slow and difficult. But it is rare to find someone whose mind combines the degrees of skill and power that Mae Chee Kaew's did. Because of that, it would be nearly impossible for the average person to match her extraordinary range of psychic perception. Those aspects of her practice will not serve as a suitable meditation guide for most practitioners.

On a more profound level, however, Mae Chee Kaew's practice points the way beyond the changing conditions of birth and death to the essence of true freedom. At the heart of that realization lies a fundamental distinction between two very different aspects of the mind: the mind's knowing essence, and the transient states of mind that arise and cease within it. By not understanding that distinction, we take those transient states to be real, to be the mind itself. In fact, they are all just changing conditions that never remain stable from one moment to the next. The knowing essence of mind is the only real constant. Mostly we lump everything together and call it mind; but actually states of mind exist in conjunction with the knowing of them. With that insight comes the realization that happiness and suffering are realities separate from the mind that knows them. The true essence of mind knows all states and all conditions, but attaches to none. Because of that, it lies beyond the shifting states of happiness and suffering. If we can see this, we can put down those conventional realities and let them go. With that understanding, liberating detachment occurs of its own accord.

Mae Chee Kaew was a countrywoman, who lived a simple village life in the northeastern region of Thailand and overcame enormous difficulties in her attempt to leave home and follow the Buddha's noble path to freedom from suffering. Her persistence, her courage, and her intuitive wisdom enabled her to transcend all conventional boundaries — both those imposed upon her by the world she lived in and those limiting her mind from within — and thereby find release from the bondage of birth and death. Although she lived and practiced under the same constraints that most women practitioners have had to endure, she embraced that challenge, skillfully harmonizing her practice to fit smoothly within the conventional monastic framework. By surrendering wholeheartedly to that time-honored system, she succeeded in turning its apparent drawbacks to her advantage. Instead of complaining of unequal status, Mae Chee Kaew diligently cultivated a mind of clear and spontaneous awareness, and thereby succeeded in cutting through her deeply-rooted delusion of personal and cultural identity. Viewed in the light of transcendent insight, the solid world of class and difference in which she had spent her entire life evaporated and disappeared.

Monks who are skilled in meditation are not biased by cultural conditioning. They have no doubt that women who observe the eight precepts and practice seriously can attain exceptionally high levels of meditation. In truth, women have a remarkable capacity for understanding Dhamma and can achieve deep levels of samādhi and develop extraordinary knowledge and wisdom. Many nuns and laywomen in Thailand surpass the monks in their accomplishments. For this reason, meditation masters generally hold female practitioners in high esteem, considering them equal to men in their spiritual potential. In the Thai forest tradition today, many revered teachers believe that women are capable of the highest spiritual attainment. They often recommend female monastics as exemplary teachers. Many forest meditation masters have women students, both nuns and laywomen, who are recognized as teachers in their own right. These women actively participate in their religious communities as skilled meditators, healers or mentors, and are revered by local people. Mae Chee Kaew was just such a woman. Practicing nuns like her have left a legacy to inspire future generations and to show how the Buddhist path of practice may be reopened by anyone, male or female.

This account of Mae Chee Kaew's life is presented in the form of a narrative biography, using the available facts placed in a historical context to tell the story of her life. I have included what information I could find to place her life in a proper setting of time and culture, citing her own words and her contemporaries' words and the known events of their time. The story I tell was compiled from various Thai language sources. I am deeply indebted to Ajaan Mahā Boowa who, through his spoken and written teachings, related many key stories about her meditation practice. I have used his lucid descriptions of the transcendent levels of insight and wisdom to work out the details of Mae Chee Kaew's step by step progression to enlightenment. She was one of Ajaan Mahā Boowa's most gifted disciples, and he has left us no doubt about her spiritual attainments.

Ajaan Intawai was an important inspiration for writing this book. Having enjoyed a close relationship with Mae Chee Kaew since childhood, he proved to be a valuable source of cultural background and historical detail. Mae Chee Kaew's surviving relatives provided intimate accounts of her family life, as well as the early years of her renunciation of worldly affairs. Dr. Pensri Makaranon, who nursed her tirelessly in old age, has shared a vivid recollection of Mae Chee Kaew's final years, including many of the fascinating stories Mae Chee Kaew herself related to her medical attendants.

All of this material I have stitched together to weave the fabric of her life. However, many irreconcilable gaps and inconsistencies appeared in the different written and verbal accounts. I found multiple versions of the same story and in some instances crucial details are missing. So I have also resorted to my imagination to fill out the picture of her life and her practice, adding graphic details to fashion a vibrant and clear mental image of the woman and her extraordinary achievements. This is not a work of scholarship so much as a narrative biography that is intended to provide a source of inspiration to those who are devoted to Buddhist practice. With that purpose in mind, it is hoped that this book will be viewed mainly as an invitation to contemplate the depths and subtleties of mind that are experienced on the Buddha's path to total liberation.

Part One
Blessing

Having been born, we attach importance to the passing days, months and years; we believe in the importance of our lives and the lives of others. For that reason, our minds are constantly concerned with pain and suffering.

Moonstone Pearls

Beginning in the 9th century, the migration of the Tai people from southern China progressed as steadily and quietly as the flow of monsoon floodwaters that seep into dense forests and blanket fertile plains, changing color with the hue of the sky and form with the contour of the land. Woven together geographically, Tai ethnic groups of common origins and similar culture spread over mountains and down valleys from south China into ancient Siam.

Among the many Tai sub-groups were the Phu Tai people, who were fiercely independent farmers and hunters. Originating from the Chinese prefecture of Jiaozhi on the banks of the Red River, they were driven by a succession of political upheavals to forge their way south through the neighboring Lao kingdoms, gradually pushed further with each generation until they reached the banks of the Mekong River. They settled inland and remained there for centuries, migrating later to more fertile land on the river's opposite side and fanning out along its western territories.

Over centuries of struggle and hardship — through droughts, floods, natural disasters and communal tragedies — the resourceful Phu Tai people were eventually united into a cohesive political entity ruled by a hereditary local lord and a powerful clan of warriors and administrators. The kingdom of Mukdahan — named for the moonstone pearls, or *mukda*, which the Phu Tai discovered in local streambeds — became a regional center for their traditional way of life.

Baan Huay Sai was a small Phu Tai farming community in the Kham Cha-ee district of old Siam's Mukdahan province. Situated at the far edge of the Mekong River flood plain, where the southern range of the Phu Phan mountains rise to form a rolling landscape, the village perched neatly on a smooth stretch of high ground between the Huay Bang Sai and Huay Bang Ee rivers. It was a settlement of rustic wooden houses, built on stilts and shaded by large overhanging trees, as though the living space had been carved out of a dense primeval forest. The villagers were country people with rough, unrefined manners and simple guileless lives, sustained by subsistence farming and the hunting of wild game. They cultivated rice, each family farming a plot of fertile land on the village outskirts that had been cleared of trees. Beyond the clearing, lay a thick jungle terrain. Teeming with tigers and elephants, this vast forest was believed to harbor hidden dangers and frightening places, compelling the inhabitants to band together in village settlements for safety and companionship.

Situated over a large expanse of fertile territory along the Mekong, Mukdahan began as a separate kingdom and later evolved into a semi-autonomous principality, owing allegiance to Siam's Chakri Dynasty.

Legend has it that Baan Huay Sai village was once home to three royal sisters — Princess Kaew, Princess Klum and Princess Kah — who, through the female line, stamped a lasting imprint on the Phu Tai character. By the force of their personalities, they instilled in generations of offspring a sharp intellect, an implacable determination and a fair-minded viewpoint. Proud of their heritage and independent in spirit, the Phu Tai were unified by the bonds of tradition, custom and language. These bonds were passed down like sacred trusts from one generation to the next.

In late 19th century Siam, the local magistrate of Baan Huay Sai village was Tason Sianglum. Tason's authority came from *jao meung*, the provincial lord who had appointed him. His responsibilities were to mediate local disputes, moderate local tempers, and engage his fellow Phu Tai's innate sense of justice in order to preserve neighborly peace and harmony.

Magistrate Tason was a fair-minded man of simple wisdom who resolved to serve his people well. By maintaining communal peace, he was doing his part to maintain the traditional Phu Tai identity. His wife, Don, was a gentle and kind woman who carried the title of magistrate as well, but had no public duties as such. Instead, she raised a family of five children. The oldest three were boys, followed in quick succession by two girls. The youngest was born early on the morning of November 8, 1901. Her mother named her Tapai, which meant "eye-catching".

From an early age, Tapai had an aura of mystery about her, as though she knew more than she could ever express. When she was old enough to speak, she giggled with delight as she whispered to her mother about nocturnal adventures in which she accompanied glow-ing globes of light to wondrous places — places she could describe only with gestures and not with words. Many years later, after she became a Buddhist nun, she would recount how she grew up, befriended by celestial playmates, *devas* of the heavenly spheres whose radiant forms only she could see. They had been her spiritual companions in countless past lives, and they worried that her spirit might succumb to the attractions of physical embodiment. To prevent her spirit from becoming anchored in the earthly plane, the *devas* often enticed Tapai to separate herself from her physical body to tour the spiritual realm of celestial abodes with them.

Tapai's father and mother were both devout Buddhists who showed enlightened tendencies. For instance, they maintained a respectful distance from the practice of spirit worship that was common in Phu Tai culture. The family lived just behind the village temple, their property located along the bamboo fence which enclosed the temple compound, so close that the big mango tree shading the temple's perimeter dropped ripe fruit into Tapai's family yard each summer. In this surrounding, Tapai grew up attuned to the mellow sounds of chanting, morning and evening, and acquainted with the daily rhythms of monastic life. Already as a child, she learned to focus her mind by concentrating on the monks' soft, mesmerizing cadence until it resonated inside her heart. She was thrilled by the excitement of festival days that punctuated the Buddhist calendar year, when the whole village gathered to celebrate in the temple fairgrounds behind her house.

Tapai observed how her father treated the monks with great respect. It was not the kind of tense, guarded respect he showed to high-ranking officials. It was, instead, a natural, open deference, full of warmth and devotion. Each morning, after Tapai and her mother placed their offerings of sticky rice and curries, wrapped in banana leaf, into the monks' alms bowls, her father followed the monks to the edge of the village. Tason always kept a respectful distance as the monks received their daily offerings and helped carry the food-laden bowls back to the temple. On the four religious observance days of each month — the days of the new and full moons and the two days of the half-moon — Tason scrupulously maintained the precepts while enjoying the luxury of spending a whole day at the temple, chatting and doing odd jobs for the monks.

As a young child, Tapai's life energy moved freely between her physical world and her spiritual world. Then, suddenly, when she was five years old, both worlds collapsed. Without thought or warning — before the possibility ever crossed her mind or entered her imagination — her mother fell ill and died. In her shock and confusion, everything she believed in crumbled and fell apart.

At the simple funeral ceremony, Tapai stared on, gripped by fear at seeing her mother's cold, stiff body, wrapped in layers of white cloth, lying atop a crude pyre of logs and branches. When the flames leapt up and tore through the cloth and skin to expose raw, blistering flesh and twisted sinews, she turned her head away in pain. Even as the fire finally came to rest, and all that remained were ashes and charred bones, she still could not bear to look.

With her mother's death, Tapai learned at an early age that change and loss are part of life; that life is inseparable from pain and death. Gradually, with the help of her family — especially her two brothers, P'On and P'In — she began to heal. The boys loved their sister — she with her bright eyes and strong will. Although they too were in pain over the loss of their mother, the brothers constantly tried to cheer Tapai up and lighten her mood. Finally, however, it was a new, closer, more personal relationship with her father that ultimately lifted her heart and cleared away the burden of grief.

After his wife's death, Tason began taking Tapai to the temple on lunar observance days. She sat with her father for hours, watching, listening, daydreaming — but, most of all, healing. She grew so fond of the temple atmosphere that whenever she had free time she liked to sneak into the grounds, sit beneath the mango tree, and do nothing but enjoy a sense of calm.

Tapai liked to celebrate Visākha Pūjā, the May festival honoring the Buddha's birth, enlightenment and passing away. May in Baan Huay Sai village was one of the most beautiful months of the year. With the first showers of the annual rains, flowers burst into bloom, bringing small explosions of color everywhere and armloads of blossoms for offerings at the festival. Flowers were gathered in abundance and placed lovingly around the radiant shrine of the Buddha with its multi-tiered altar. In the evening, a candle-lit procession of monks and laity would wind its way around the ordination hall; after which, the monks led the entire congregation in chanting ancient verses of praise for the Lord Buddha and his teaching. The chants were deeply inspiring and so moving that they lifted the participants from the commonplace of daily existence to a higher, more exalted plane.

As the spiritual bond between father and daughter deepened, Tapai began, hesitantly at first, to tell him about her other world, her inner world of mystery and surprise. Tason listened patiently, quizzically, to tales of playful deities and dream-world escapades —

flights of fantasy which he tolerated, but to which he was careful to lend no credence.

Then, at age seven, Tapai started to experience vivid recollections of her past lives, both human and nonhuman. Innocently and eagerly, she described to her father the lifetimes she had recalled, spontaneously, as if from a vision: the life of a chicken, a doctor, a princess, a commoner. Tapai's father had never been pleased with her clairvoyance and his growing disapproval showed. His mood shifted dramatically. His complexion darkened and a new note — a threatening tone — entered his voice. He warned her — at first, gently, and then later, more sternly — not to mention these visions to anyone; otherwise, she would risk being labeled crazy, or worse. He worried that such a stigma might become irrevocably attached to her as she grew up in that small rural community.

Gradually, Tapai adjusted to her new family situation by assuming the traditional responsibilities of a woman's work. With her older sister, Tapai shared the burden of housekeeping. Being the stronger and more willful of the two, Tapai resolved to perfect the countless little chores that she had seen her mother perform so gracefully. Somebody had to rise early to kindle the fire and steam the family's daily rice. Somebody was needed to set out the meal, wash the pots and put away the saucers. There was sweeping, scrubbing and washing to be done; cotton to be spun, cloth to be woven and clothes to be mended. Brooms were hand-crafted, and so were an assortment of baskets — woven bamboo ones for packing sticky rice and plaited rattan ones for collecting wild mushrooms and forest greens.

Training her body resolutely to adapt to its new tasks, Tapai became adept in all these numerous duties at a young age. Each chore, each handicraft required special skill, and hours of tedious practice to master. When she wasn't practicing these tasks at home, she was working in the rice fields or the adjacent forests acquiring other skills. Her mother used to take her on excursions into the surrounding hills to pick wild herbs and forest greens, or to fish in the outlying ponds. Now she went with her aunts and cousins, learning how to distinguish edible mushrooms from poisonous ones, the sweet herbs from the bitter. Whether it was planting, harvesting, or simply gathering, food was always a daily concern.

Rice — the sticky, glutinous variety that was the Phu Tai staple — held a steady and inescapable sway over the villagers, influencing the tenor of their lives. In anticipation of the annual rains, farmers sprouted seedlings in small plots of land while their water buffaloes plowed the fields. When the rains finally came and saturated the ground with sufficient downpours, the fields were trampled by the buffaloes into coarse mud, creating a rich bog for planting the rice sprouts. Then, groups of women, bent at the waist and walking backwards, grabbed handfuls of young seedlings to thrust in small bunches into the thick mud, planting several strands at a time while trying to keep the rows straight.

Rice farming was exhausting labor, but it created close-knit village communities. After Tapai's mother died, all the women in her extended family worked together during the planting season to cultivate her father's fields. While she was still too young to do hard labor, Tapai often stood on the embankment under gray skies and watched the women sloshing through the wet soft earth, eager for the day when she would take her place alongside them.

After several years, and a respectable interval of mourning, Tapai's father remarried. His new bride was a young widow whose husband had died in one of the epidemics that periodically disrupted the regularity of village existence, adding another layer of hardship to an already harsh life. Tapai liked her step-mother. They enjoyed each other's company immediately; and Tapai gained a new companion in the woman's young daughter. It felt like a new beginning, and Tapai was happy again. She met every situation with a ready smile; and the hardships of rural life seemed to evaporate in the presence of her bright and cheerful demeanor.

But, when her baby half-brother died shortly after birth, Tapai felt the pain of loss and grieved once more. She experienced again the bitter truth of impermanence — knowledge that she seemed destined to learn in her world of constant change and loss. She saw that the world around her fell apart only to renew itself everyday and with every season. Change was such a persistent fact of life, that parting became simply an ordinary part of living.

Phu Tai villagers led hard lives. Women's work was endless: cooking, washing, sewing, weaving, and sowing and harvesting the rice crop — year in and year out. It helped Tapai that she got along well with her step-mother. They developed a close working relationship, sharing heavy work and lighthearted moments with equal good humor. Tapai found help of other kinds as well. Without a local school, Tapai could not get formal education. She found, instead, that her home, the rice fields and the wild forests were her school. In these places she received instruction that can only be seen as enduring and essential in life: lessons in love, renunciation, change and patience; lessons in disappointment and determination; and lessons in suffering and equanimity. With this schooling, her childhood education progressed, year upon year.

Know yourself, accept your faults and work
to overcome them. Hide nothing from yourself.
Above all, don't lie to yourself. You can lie to
the entire world if you like, but you must never
lie to yourself.

Fearless Warrior Spirit

From time to time during the dry and hot seasons of the year,
wandering *dhutanga* monks passed through Baan Huay Sai, searching
for secluded places to camp and meditate in solitude. The mountains
and forests surrounding the village were areas of vast wilderness, for-
bidding and inhospitable. Wild animals roamed freely, and malevolent
spirits were believed to reign supreme. The terrain remained a jungle,
and fear kept it remote and sequestered. This made it an ideal place
for wandering meditation monks to live and practice their ascetic way
of life in solitude.

Detached, reserved and intent on renunciation, *dhutanga* monks
hiked through the wilderness, often alone, along deserted trails. They
sought secluded locations that offered body and mind a calm, quiet
setting — a ridge, a cave, an overhanging cliff — places suitable for
striving to attain the end of all suffering. Living a life entirely out-
of-doors, the *dhutanga* monk constantly put himself at the mercy of

the elements and the vagaries of the weather. Living in harmony with his natural surroundings, a *dhutanga* monk's daily life featured nature's rich diversity: rocks and trees, rivers and streams, tigers, snakes, elephants and bears. For his livelihood, he depended on collecting alms food in the small settlements that had sprung up at the jungle's edge.

The Phu Tai felt a common bond with the wandering ascetics and their fearless warrior spirit. Because of that, the monks easily found support for their lifestyle in Phu Tai communities. Tapai's father was especially fond of the forest monks: "True sons of the Buddha" he called them, with an appreciative smile. Energized by seeing them, he welcomed their arrival with childlike enthusiasm.

In 1914, the arrival of Ajaan Sao Kantasīlo — the renowned *dhutanga* master — transformed the spiritual landscape of Baan Huay Sai village life forever. Having come from afar, he and a small band of disciples simply wandered into the area on foot one day. They had been hiking for months, first crossing the Mekong River from Laos to Siam's Nakhon Phanom province, then trekking over the eastern hills of Sakon Nakhon and down through the Phu Phan wilderness to reach Mukdahan.

Though he was 55 years old, Ajaan Sao walked entire days in the tropical heat, crossing the most arduous terrain with steady, effortless steps. When he and his group reached the vicinity of Baan Huay Sai village, the annual rains were just beginning. Cloud bursts and cooling showers were followed by lustrous sunshine illuminating the sky, while damp heat hugged the ground. Ajaan Sao knew that the changing climate beckoned him to search for a suitable site to spend the rains retreat, an annual three-month period of intensive meditation.

Following the Buddha's instructions, monks cease their wandering for the duration of the monsoon season to reside in one location, under the protection of a roof.

Ajaan Sao was first spotted in the humid, misty dawn when he entered the sleepy village, leading a column of figures dressed in ochre-colored robes. Walking barefoot and with an alms bowl slung across one shoulder, the monks appeared ready to receive what generosity the inhabitants had to offer: rice, pickled fish, bananas, smiles and respectful bows. Stirred by the monks' serene, dignified appearance, the women, men and children of the village scrambled to find some food to offer the "Dhamma monks", all the while yelling back and forth to one another in their excitement. By the time Ajaan Sao and his monks walked past Tapai's house, her whole family stood expectantly along the dirt track at the front, waiting to place morsels of food in the monks' bowls, and hoping to accumulate special merit by their actions.

Eager to discover the identity of the new arrivals, Tapai's father along with a few friends followed the monks back to their temporary campsite in the nearby foothills. Although Ajaan Sao was venerated as a supreme master throughout the region, Tason and his friends had never met him face to face. Surprise turned into joy and excitement when they heard his name mentioned. Tapai's father resolved to have Ajaan Sao settle in the area, if only for the duration of the monsoon season. Well acquainted with the local terrain — fast-flowing streams and winding rivers, overhanging caves and rocky outcrops, open savannah and dense jungle — Tason acted as a guide to the venerable master, proposing various retreat sites for the coming rains. He was relieved, then overjoyed, when Ajaan Sao chose to enter the retreat at Banklang Cave, situated in a forested area scattered with flat, out-spread sandstone boulders about an hour's walk from the village.

Long before their introduction to Buddhism, the Phu Tai people upheld an ancient tradition of ritual spirit worship. They paid obei-sance and performed sacrifices to benevolent ancestral spirits, and to the guardian spirits of the forests. Ancestor worship was so ingrained in their character that the spirit shrine became a central feature of home life. Families presented daily oblations to placate long-dead forbearers, actions believed to protect the family, the house, even the village, from unpleasant occurrences — including the unpleasant con-sequences of neglecting that sacred duty. If things went well, that meant the spirits were happy with the family's efforts. Neglecting the rituals displeased the spirits, which accounted for why things went wrong. Auspicious days were sought for the start of every endeavor and propitiatory offerings were made to win the favor of local deities. The deities of earth and sky were not omitted. Due to an intimate as-sociation with rice and water, the Phu Tai inherited an age-old saying: "In eating, don't forget the rice-field spirit. And never overlook the water spirit that brings us fish".

So, while the center of each village featured the Buddhist temple, or *wat*, spirit worship still dominated a major portion of the villagers' lives. For years, Ajaan Sao wandered through the countryside, enlight-ening the locals about the virtues of moral behavior and explaining the causal consequences of their actions and beliefs. Ajaan Sao did not deny the existence of spirits and deities. They abided everywhere, in everything — forests, trees, mountains, caves, rivers, fields, earth and sky — and he was tolerant of belief in nonphysical existence. What he opposed was the belief that such entities were the causes, the instigators, of human pain and suffering; and the belief that bribes of sacrificial offerings could guard against adversity and misfortune.

Local deities and ghosts were as much a part of Phu Tai village life as the sun, the rain and the morning fog; as inescapable as birth, life and death. This Ajaan Sao did not refute. But he taught them that every nonphysical being experienced the karmic consequences of its own actions; each was the product of its own *kamma*, just like the villagers themselves. Worshipping these beings was, in effect, attributing to them a power that they did not possess. The essence of Ajaan Sao's message was personal responsibility. Pleasure or pain, happiness or suffering, having or lacking: all are a result of an individual's past karmic deeds, combined with one's moral behavior in the present.

Preparing Ajaan Sao's encampment for the retreat required the construction of shelters to weather the monsoon rains: a single-room hut for each monk and a central *sala* for meals and recitations of the monastic rules. Paths for walking meditation needed leveling and latrines needed digging. With joy in his heart and a bounce in his step, Tapai's father quickly volunteered his services — cutting and sawing trees for stout posts, splitting and pressing bamboo for floors and walls, collecting and binding tall grasses for roof thatching. Paths were cleared, graded and swept; outdoor toilets were excavated and encircled with thatch. By the time Tason and his friends completed the work, a small, orderly forest monastery had been crafted from the jungle wilderness.

Spiritual transformation happened gradually for the Phu Tai village. First one family, then another, took the leap of faith — faith in the protective power of the Lord Buddha and faith in their own moral virtue. Many burned their spirit shrines and objects of ritual worship to ashes. Some were skeptical of Buddhism, and hesitated. Who knew how the local deities would react. Might they not take revenge?

Naturally frugal with speech, Ajaan Sao used his words sparingly to counter common fears and inculcate faith and virtue among the villagers. In talks that were direct and easy to understand, he taught them simple lessons. To instill faith, he encouraged them to replace the custom of sacrificial offerings with the practice of taking refuge in the Buddha, Dhamma and Sangha. To inculcate virtue, he encouraged them to observe the five moral precepts: refraining from killing, stealing, lying, committing adultery and taking intoxicants. The villagers learned that by guarding their minds and actions with simple, yet potent practices, and thus avoiding behavior harmful to themselves and others, they would acquire the means to protect themselves.

So as to help them overcome and rid themselves of fear, Ajaan Sao taught them the protective power of meditation. First, he guided people in paying homage to the Buddha by chanting the Blessed One's virtues in unison. Once their hearts were calm and clear, he proceeded to allay their doubts and worries, speaking simply and concisely: "Don't be afraid. As long as you meditate, focusing on 'buddho, buddho, buddho', the spirits will never disturb you. Everyone falls ill at some point in life. But it's nonsense to think that sickness is caused by ghosts and spirits. Our bodies are constantly decaying and renewing themselves. The human body and illness go hand in hand. It's pointless to ask your dead relatives for help. Far better that you practice meditation and dedicate the merit of your actions to their spirits. Then you both will gain some benefit."

As custom dictated, the villagers — especially devout Buddhists — reserved part of each lunar observance day for religious activities. They went to the monastery to offer food, help with the chores, listen to Dhamma teachings, practice meditation or undertake a combination of these activities. Tapai, now 13 years old, often accompanied her parents on early morning hikes to the forest monastery at Banklang Cave. Being a girl, however, she was not allowed to mingle with the monks. So, when Ajaan Sao spoke to the laypeople, Tapai sat far in the back of the *sala*, just within earshot of his soft, mellow voice.

Seated behind the women and peering over her step-mother's shoulder, Tapai absorbed the atmosphere and the teachings. She, like all the villagers, had inherited the local cultural beliefs as a matter of course. Her worldview was colored by the same historical background. Yet, though she knew of the existence of spirits since early childhood, Tapai was not a superstitious person. She preferred instead to seek cause and effect relationships by means of common sense. So, while her family kept a small shrine honoring the spirits, Tapai's natural inclination was to embrace the Buddha and the truth of his teaching.

Thus, from an early age, Tapai felt the lasting influence of Ajaan Sao. She responded to his simple, down-to-earth manner, his even, serene temperament, and his noble and dignified appearance. He inspired a deep devotion in her and left an indelible impression with his character, his words, his very presence. Even though she did not really make an effort to focus her mind in meditation as he instructed, Tapai sensed in her heart that Ajaan Sao had attained perfect peace. Soon, Tapai felt the subtle force of Ajaan Sao's personality pulling her in a new direction.

She first felt this pull on one memorable occasion. She heard Ajaan Sao praise the womenfolk for their generous support of the monks. Their daily offerings of food and other necessities were not only beneficial to the monks, but they were also a blessing for their own futures as well. He then added, briefly and emphatically, that the virtue of generosity was nothing compared to the virtue of re-nunciation practiced by white-robed nuns meditating in the forest. This remark stirred Tapai at the core of her being. The nuns, said Ajaan Sao, were a fruitful field of merit for all living beings. With that pointed pronouncement, Ajaan Sao had planted a small seed in the young girl's heart that would one day grow into a majestic Bodhi tree.

Don't doubt the value of meditation or underestimate your abilities. Be content with whatever
progress you make because it reflects a part of
the truth you are seeking. As such, it is something you can rely on.

Blessing of a Lifetime

Ajaan Sao spent three years living in the vicinity of Baan Huay
Sai village, first in one forest location, then in another. By the time
he departed Kham Cha-ee district and wandered north, the religious
landscape in the area had been altered for good. So influential was
Ajaan Sao, that most of the locals now favored Buddhist practices
over spirit worship.

Tapai's father had accompanied Ajaan Sao as he moved to different places in the area, suggesting new secluded spots and working
with his friends to construct small bamboo shelters for him and his
disciples. As much as anyone, he was pleased by the Buddhist renais-
sance spreading through the community. While Tapai's father was
saddened to see Ajaan Sao leave, he was simultaneously consoled
by his knowledge that Buddhism was now firmly established in the
hearts and minds of his Phu Tai neighbors. Little did he suspect,

though, that Ajaan Sao's departure would be succeeded by the arrival of the most revered Buddhist master of them all.

Ajaan Mun Bhūridatto was a legend in the making. The story of his life and spiritual attainments were to gain an exalted status unparalleled in modern Thai history. Already his sterling reputation had reached the northeastern provinces, passed on by word-of-mouth throughout the region. It was said that he expounded the profound nature of Dhamma with such power and persuasion that even the spirits were subdued in his presence. *Devas, nāgas, garudas* and *asuras* were all captivated by the aura of his abiding love and compassion. His austere way of life had made him a master of the ascetic, a pioneer of the *dhutanga* lifestyle. His disciples, the monks who lived by his example, had become his legion, and he guided them with the uncompromising discipline of a consummate spiritual warrior. It was rumored that by meeting Ajaan Mun only once, one would be bestowed with a lifetime of good fortune.

A true wanderer, Ajaan Mun rarely stayed in the same location for more than one rains retreat. After the rains ended, he and his monks roamed freely, unburdened, through the vast northeastern wilderness, like birds at ease, flying peacefully to wherever the wind took them. Like birds, who soar freely and are content to land in a tree, pond or marsh; then to fly off and leave all behind with no lingering attachment, so too did *dhutanga* monks lead lives of sublime detachment.

Thus, in 1917, as the annual monsoon season was fast approaching, Ajaan Mun and a group of sixty monks wandered down from the north to arrive in the wooded foothills overlooking the village of Baan Huay Sai. They camped under trees, in caves, under overhanging cliffs and in nearby charnel grounds. Following Ajaan Sao's ground-breaking path into the Baan Huay Sai community, Ajaan Mun's arrival caused a stir of excitement. The villagers were thrilled with the prospect of making merit by supporting monks. The entire village of Baan Huay Sai welcomed the Dhamma monks with faith and gratitude.

Ajaan Mun and his disciples took up their practice in their new surroundings, living simply and practicing meditation in the *dhutanga* tradition. Many villagers flocked to the hillside encampment on lunar observance days, and Tapai's parents made sure to join them. At that time, Tapai was hardly aware of Ajaan Mun's distinguished reputation. She had heard his name mentioned in connection with Ajaan Sao — the two had long been close spiritual companions, supporting and encouraging each other in the way of practice. That much Tapai knew, but little else. Accompanying her parents from time to time, she noticed differences between Ajaan Mun and Ajaan Sao. She saw at once that Ajaan Mun's forceful, dynamic character contrasted sharply with Ajaan Sao's serene and even temperament. Physically, Ajaan Mun was shorter and more slender than Ajaan Sao; but when he spoke, he was much more active: his arms flew, his hands gestured dramatically, and his voice thundered.

Tapai felt a little afraid of Ajaan Mun at first; a little wary of his intensity. In the village each morning, as she placed offerings of food in his alms bowl, Ajaan Mun frequently stopped and addressed her directly, encouraging her to come see him more often. But, feeling shy and timid in his presence, Tapai only dared to go on special religious days when she was with her parents and a group of the local villagers. Ajaan Mun was always exceptionally kind to her, often recognizing her presence on observance days and exchanging a few words with her. Knowing intuitively that she possessed uncommon spiritual potential and deep devotion, he began encouraging her to do meditation. He explained to her the same basic technique that Ajaan Sao had taught: silent repetition of the meditation-word 'buddho', practiced repeatedly and continuously until it became the sole object of her awareness. He emphasized that mindfulness — being mindful and aware only of the moment-to-moment recitation of each syllable, bud-dho, bud-dho — must be present to direct her efforts: it would make her alert and fully attentive to the rise and fall of each repetition. A simple method, she thought; but, due to instinctive modesty, she hesitated taking it up at first.

As Ajaan Mun repeatedly insisted that she try meditation practice, Tapai began to suspect that she must possess some inherent ability. She thought to herself: "I am just an ordinary village girl, but, I must have some inherent virtue. Why else would he show such an interest in me? From now on, I should take his advice and try to practice meditation in the way he has so kindly taught me."

One evening, after dinner, Tapai readied herself and went to her bedroom early. All day, she had felt a willful determination welling up inside her heart: today was the day to focus her full attention on the repetition of buddho, just as Ajaan Mun had taught her. With devotion and a serious sense of purpose, Tapai began to mentally repeat the meditation-word buddho. After about fifteen minutes of steady, deliberate recitation, her conscious mind suddenly dropped down to the heart and converged into a profound state of quiet stillness. It was as though she had instantly fallen to the bottom of a well, where her body and mind vanished into silence. The experience was so new, and so extraordinary, that she had no idea what had happened to her.

After a brief time, her mind withdrew slightly from deep samādhi, and she became uncomfortably aware of an image of her body lying dead in front of her. She recognized her own corpse very clearly. The image was so real, and so vivid in detail, that it convinced her she must have died. Suddenly, seemingly out of nowhere, an anxious thought ruffled the calm: "Since I'm dead, who'll take my place cooking rice to put into the monks' bowls tomorrow? Who's going to tell Ajaan Mun that I died sitting in meditation tonight?"

Quickly suppressing these worries, Tapai steadied her mind and accepted her fate. She mused: "If I'm dead, I'm dead! Everyone in the world is bound to die. Nobody can escape from death. Even a great king must die one day."

Her mind then became resolute and focused as she fixed her attention to the dead body lying prostrate before her. The image had not faded or changed in the least, which reinforced her impression that she was actually dead. As she pondered the consequences of her death without reaching any conclusions, a small group of local villagers appeared in her vision. They simply materialized in the picture, slowly picked up her limp, lifeless body and carried it to a nearby charnel ground. As the villagers laid her body in the middle of the desolate area, she noticed Ajaan Mun and a group of monks solemnly walking toward the corpse. Ajaan Mun stopped in front of it and gazed down for a moment before turning to the monks to say: "This girl is dead. Now I'll perform the funeral rites."

As the monks looked on impassively, heads slightly bowed, Ajaan Mun softly intoned the funeral chant: "*Aniccā vata saṅkhārā...*"

"When the components that make up the body have died, the body is no longer of use. The heart, however, does not die; it goes on working ceaselessly. When it develops in the way of virtue, its benefits are unlimited. But if it is used in harmful ways, it becomes a danger to oneself."

With calm deliberation, Ajaan Mun slowly repeated this dictum three times in succession. Standing tall and perfectly still, except for the movement of his arm, he tapped her corpse three times with his walking stick, declaring with each tap:

"The body does not last; having been born, it must die. The heart, however, does last. It is never born, and it does not die when the body dies. It is constantly in motion, spinning and shifting, following the causes and conditions that lead it on."

Continuing to tap the corpse rhythmically with the tip of his walking stick, Ajaan Mun appeared to reiterate this truth over and over again. With each gentle tap of his stick, her body started to decompose. First the skin blistered and peeled, exposing the flesh beneath. Further tapping rotted the flesh and sinews, revealing the bones and inner organs. Entranced, Tapai watched passively as her entire body quickly decayed, until only the hard bones remained intact. Placing his hand in the skeletal debris and picking up the "kernel" of the heart in his palm, Ajaan Mun announced:

"The heart can never be destroyed. If it were destroyed, you would never regain consciousness."

Tapai witnessed the unfolding of the entire scene with a mixture of awe and trepidation. She was not sure how to understand it. When

Ajaan Mun finished speaking, she puzzled: "If the whole body decomposes at death, leaving only the bones behind, what is it that regains consciousness?"

Still looking at the kernel in his hand and without lifting his gaze, Ajaan Mun immediately answered her thought: "It's bound to return! How could you not regain consciousness when the kernel that brings it back is still there? You will regain consciousness tomorrow morning at dawn."

Tapai spent the entire night seated in meditation, completely absorbed in the vision of her dead body. Only at the first light of dawn did her mind withdraw from deep samādhi. As she was becoming aware of herself, she looked down at her body, seated on the bed. She realized, with a sigh of relief, that she had not died. Her normal waking state had returned, and she felt pleased to be alive. But, then, as she pondered the night's events, she began to chide herself for falling asleep and dreaming throughout the night when she should have been meditating instead. She was sure that Ajaan Mun would be disappointed with her.

Later in the morning, Ajaan Mun passed by her house on his daily almsround. As Tapai placed food in his alms bowl, he looked at her quizzically; then, he smiled and told her to come see him when he had finished eating. Her father accompanied her on the familiar walk to Ajaan Mun's encampment, unsure why she was asked to go. Could there be a problem? Tapai walked silently, brooding and feeling ashamed of herself for falling asleep in meditation. What was she going to tell Ajaan Mun? Certainly he'd be displeased. She wanted to hide, but she didn't know where, or how.

As soon as they entered the encampment, Tapai mumbled some excuse to her father and rushed off to help the womenfolk fetch water at the stream. Seeing Tason approaching alone, Ajaan Mun looked surprised and asked him for Tapai's whereabouts. Tason then quickly fetched his daughter from the stream.

Nervous and uneasy, Tapai crawled to where Ajaan Mun was seated and bowed down three times before him. Immediately, before she had time to draw a breath, he asked her, "How was your meditation last night?" Timidly and awkwardly, she replied, "It was just hopeless, sir. After repeating *buddho* for about fifteen minutes, I felt my mind drop down a deep well. After that, I fell asleep and dreamed all night long. When I awoke at dawn, I was so disappointed with my meditation that I still can't get over it. I'm really worried you'll scold me for my lack of effort."

Upon hearing this, Ajaan Mun laughed with joy and asked her straightaway, "How did you sleep? And what did you dream? Please tell me about it."

When she told him what had happened, he roared with laughter. Delighted by her story, he said, "That was not sleep! You were not dreaming! What you experienced was the calm, integrated state called samādhi. Remember this well. What you thought was a dream was really a vision arising spontaneously from the deep concentration of samādhi. If you have any further experiences of this kind, just relax and allow them to happen. There is no need to be worried or frightened. I don't want you to be afraid, but you must remain alert and fully aware of whatever takes place in your meditation. As long as I am living here, no harm will come to you. But from now on, please come and tell me about the visions that you experience in your meditation."

Cultivate your mind, as a farmer cultivates his fields. Gradually clear the land; prepare the soil; plough the rows; sow the seeds; spread the manure; water the plants and pull the weeds. Eventually, you'll reap a golden harvest.

The Mulberry Grove

Tapai spent her formative, teenage years working hard. Diligent and energetic by nature, she always worked on her own initiative without needing to be coaxed or coerced. One year when the harvest was complete and the raw grain was safely stored away, she eagerly embarked on the planting of a mulberry grove.

The Phu Tai specialized in raising silkworms for the sake of turning the raw silk strands from their cocoons into thread and fabric, and mulberry leaves were the silkworm's main diet. Once a mulberry tree's fruit ripened, its leaves were cut and spread out inside wide, shallow baskets full of silkworms. Tapai knew that a grove of mulberry trees would be a profitable resource, providing an additional source of livelihood for her family.

Tapai had learned about silkworm farming from her step-mother and now intended to produce her own independent source of mulberry leaves. Tapai took pleasure in clearing a patch of high ground at the far end of her family's field, a large knoll of partially forested land suitable for a Mulberry grove. Working diligently, she cleared and leveled the ground. In the flat clearings, surrounded by shady hardwood trees that protected the saplings from the harsh sun, Tapai planted the mulberry trees. She tended them carefully until they took firm root and began to flourish in the damp tropical heat. As soon as the trees in her grove matured, she planned to begin raising silkworms.

Not long thereafter, Tapai overheard Ajaan Mun explaining to the villagers that he was looking for a suitable place to spend the rains retreat. He wanted a broad stretch of high ground where the foliage was not too dense, and where the earth had some exposure to the drying heat of the sun, so that the dampness would not become too oppressive during the long, wet monsoon season. Tapai immediately thought of her mulberry grove. It rose above the rice fields on a hillock allowing the rainwater to drain away easily. The breezes off the rice fields helped blow away the humidity and keep the area cool. The level clearings, where she had planted the mulberry trees, were suitable for building bamboo huts; and the forest trees provided adequate seclusion.

After consulting with her father and her brothers, she invited Ajaan Mun to visit her property so that he could see its suitability for himself. When Ajaan Mun showed delight and satisfaction with the environment, she smiled joyfully and prepared to beg the great master to accept the land as a gift and, out of compassion for her, to spend the rains retreat there. But, before she could open her mouth to speak, he declared loudly for all to hear that the grove was precisely the kind of place he needed to build a small monastery for the coming rains. Taken by surprise at first, Tapai forgot to speak, as though everything was settled and nothing further needed to be said. Ajaan Mun turned to her with a quizzical smile. In her heart, the mulberry grove already belonged to him, they both knew that. All that remained was a formal offer from her. Tapai quickly bowed to her knees, prostrated three times at his feet and begged him to kindly accept the piece of land as a gift from her entire family. Ajaan Mun nodded his assent and blessed her generosity. He assured her that, by the fruit of the merit she had just made, she would never be poor in her lifetime.

Ajaan Mun's new monastery was called Wat Nong Nong, taking its name from a nearby low-lying swamp. Led by Tapai's father, the village men quickly got to work, felling and sawing small tress and cutting and splitting bamboo to construct simple huts for Ajaan Mun and his disciples. Ajaan Mun allowed only twelve monks to live with him at Wat Nong Nong during the rains, having the remainder branch out to different locations in Kham Cha-ee district with each small group living in dependence on one of the many village settlements in the area. Ajaan Mun deliberately kept his disciples spread out in separate locations that were not too close to one another but yet close enough to Wat Nong Nong so that they could easily seek his advice when encountering problems in their meditation. This arrangement suited everyone, as too many monks living in close proximity could become a hindrance to meditation.

Although the grass-roofed huts were quite small at Wat Nong Nong, the central *sala* had to be large enough to house fifty to sixty monks who would gather regularly from different locations on lunar observance days to hear recitations of the monastic rules. The village elders therefore took great care in its construction, cutting and trimming solid hardwood posts and beams to strengthen the structural framework, and raising the floor on stilts to a height of four feet to protect against flooding in heavy downpours.

Tapai was seated in the congregation at Wat Nong Nong to celebrate the first day of the rains retreat. From his elevated seat, Ajaan Mun addressed a large crowd of local supporters that spilled out of the *sala* and onto the ground below, where straw mats were spread out to accommodate them. He opened by expounding the virtues of giving, and Tapai felt a warm glow lift her heart as she recognized that her gift of land had made this inspiring occasion possible.

In a powerful, thundering voice, he explained that the real value of giving is the merit gained from acts of self-sacrifice. The most meritorious gifts are those given freely to benefit others without hoping for anything in return, other than the good results of the act of generosity itself. The spiritual qualities obtained from that charitable effort are experienced in the heart as merit and goodness. And the inspiration behind the good intention to give comes from the heart. He emphasized that it is the heart that sows the seeds of virtue, and the heart that reaps the harvest. Acts of generosity are an investment for the future for they are the foundations of a favorable rebirth.

Next, Ajaan Mun expounded the virtues of moral conduct. He explained that the moral virtue gained by faithfully observing the five moral precepts is the foundation for being a decent human being. Each of the five precepts carries a particular benefit. By refraining from harming living creatures, we can expect to enjoy good health and longevity. By refraining from stealing, our wealth and property will be safe from theft and misfortune. By refraining from adultery, partners will be faithful toward each other and live contentedly without feeling guilt or shame. By refraining from lying, we will always be trusted and respected for our integrity. By refraining from intoxicants, we will guard our intelligence and remain bright, knowledgeable people who are not easily misguided or thrown into confusion.

People who maintain a high level of moral virtue tend to reassure living beings everywhere by conveying a sense of contentment and mutual trust, and by promoting this feeling in others. The supportive and protective power of morality ensures rebirth into higher realms of existence, so those who adhere to high moral standards will surely reach a heavenly destination in their next life.

And, while such goodness comes of virtuous living, Ajaan Mun went on to explain that meditation brings the greatest rewards of all. The heart is the most important element in the whole universe; and one's material and spiritual welfare depend on the heart's well-being. He said that one lives by means of the heart. Both the contentment and the dissatisfaction one feels in this life are experienced in the heart. When one dies, one departs by means of the heart. One is reborn according to one's *kamma* — with the heart as the sole cause. Because it is the source of everything, one's heart should be trained in the right way so that one conducts oneself properly now and in the future. Through meditation, the heart can be trained correctly. By using meditation to rein in unruly thoughts, one can lay a firm foundation for spiritual calm and contentment.

For the next three months, Tapai applied herself wholeheartedly to her meditation practice. Supported by her strong faith in Ajaan Mun and nurtured by his wise counsel, her practice developed quickly. Being naturally inclined to have visions and to experience psychic phenomena, she encountered many surprising and mysterious things in her samādhi practice each night. Recognizing her inherent abilities, Ajaan Mun showed a special attentiveness to Tapai. As he sat in meditation each night, he directed the flow of his consciousness toward her to investigate her current state of mind. Thus, he was constantly aware of her meditation experiences. When he saw that her practice was exceptional on a particular night, he asked her the next day to come to see him at the monastery.

Just after dawn each morning, Tapai put food into Ajaan Mun's bowl when he walked through the village on his daily almsround. Standing in line with the other villagers, she waited as Ajaan Mun received alms food from those ahead of her. Ajaan Mun rarely spoke with anyone while walking for alms, but on days when he saw that Tapai's meditation had been especially good, he stopped as she put food in his bowl and asked her to come visit him after he finished eating. Accompanied by her family, Tapai walked to the monastery later that morning. When she began telling Ajaan Mun of her unusual experiences, the monks staying with him quickly gathered around to listen. They were eager to hear her stories about the nonphysical realms of existence, and to listen to Ajaan Mun's instructions on how to deal with them.

Ajaan Mun always gave Tapai a warmhearted welcome and listened sympathetically to everything she said. He realized that her mind inherently possessed venturesome and dynamic tendencies that easily put her in direct contact with various phenomena that the average person could not perceive. He was able to use his vast experience in these matters to give her timely and cogent advice. Soon a strong spiritual bond developed between the venerable meditation master and his young pupil. Tapai became deeply devoted to Ajaan Mun, and she felt privileged to get so much of his time and attention.

One day, shortly after the end of the annual three-month rains retreat, Ajaan Mun sent for Tapai. He told her that he and his monks would soon leave the district to continue wandering from place to place in the traditional style of *dhutanga* monks. He glanced down at her with eyebrows arched and a faint smile on his lips and asked her if she had a boyfriend. Tapai shook her head and said, no. He nodded slowly and suggested she could ordain as a white-robed renunciant and follow him on his travels, if she wished, but she must first receive her father's permission. She stared up at him, speechless, and he silently coaxed her for an answer. Groping for a deep breath, and the right words, Tapai said that she wanted to ordain and go with him, but that she feared her father would never allow it. With a reassuring smile, and a short flick of his head, Ajaan Mun sent her home.

Tapai's father gave the proposal a cold reception. He refused to grant her permission to ordain because he feared that, should his daughter later disrobe and return to lay life, she would meet difficulties in finding a husband. He urged her to enjoy a normal life and be satisfied with her lay religious practices.

Receiving the news with a knowing smile, Ajaan Mun encouraged Tapai to be patient — her time would come. Meanwhile, she had to follow his parting instructions explicitly. He forcefully insisted that she stop practicing meditation after his departure. He told her she must be content to live a worldly life for the time being. When the right time came, she would have another opportunity to develop her meditation skills. He promised her that in the future another qualified teacher would come to guide her on the right path. In the meantime, she must be patient.

Ajaan Mun saw that Tapai's mind was extremely adventurous and dynamic by nature. She did not yet have sufficient control over her mental focus to meditate safely on her own. Should something untoward occur in her meditation, she would have no one to help her in his absence. He realized that she needed a highly-skilled meditation teacher who could rein her in when she got out of hand; otherwise, she could easily go the wrong way and do damage to herself. For that reason, he forbade her to meditate after he left.

Although Tapai did not understand Ajaan Mun's reasons for this strict prohibition, she had enormous faith in him. So, she abruptly stopped her practice, even though she wanted to continue so much that she felt her heart would break. It would be another twenty years before she picked up her meditation practice again.

Your body, your mind, your life — these don't belong to you, so don't depend on them to bring true happiness.

Immersed in Endless Work

Tapai became quiet and withdrawn after Ajaan Mun's departure. The joy and the excitement that pervaded her life ebbed and disappeared when she stopped meditating. Shy by nature, Tapai was not motivated to socialize; instead she threw herself into work, which kept her constantly occupied.

Her hands were always busy; her body in constant motion. She planted cotton, combing and spinning the fluffy white balls into spools of dense thread, which she wove into fabric. She cultivated indigo trees which were then cut and crushed to extract a dark blue color to dye the cloth with. She sat at the loom for hours, teasing out spools of silk and cotton thread to weave fabric, which she meticulously cut and sewed into looped skirts and loose-fitting blouses, and then dyed in pretty patterns. She continued to plant mulberry trees to raise silkworms. She spun the raw silk thread, weaving it into coarse garments, suitable for the rigorous conditions of village life.

She showed her dexterity at basket weaving as well, shaping bamboo and rattan strands into light, durable basket-ware with artistic flair. She sewed pillows and mattresses and stuffed them with soft cotton wool. She knitted woolen clothing for the winter chill. In her spare time, she mended timeworn garments with a sharp eye and a delicate touch. She knew all the best wild herbs by sight and smell and, on daylong excursions in the cool forest, she picked handfuls of them along with wild vegetables. Returning home in the evening with baskets full, Tapai chopped and sliced her findings, then cooked the raw roots and leaves with bits of meat or fish to create a wholesome, tasty meal.

Tapai's multiple talents turned heads in the Phu Tai community. Young women with traditional skills were lauded, and considered to be exceptional brides. Besides that, she possessed other prized traits, such as stamina, dependability, loyalty to family and tradition; as well as respect for elders. Before long, suitors began to appear. One in particular, a neighborhood boy one year younger than Tapai, named Bunmaa, was emboldened to make a proposal to her parents. Still deeply moved by Ajaan Mun's teaching, Tapai showed no interest in romantic affairs and had never thought seriously of marriage. But when her parents consented to Bunmaa's proposal, she was not prepared to disobey their wishes. Perhaps it was inevitable now, part of this worldly life she must be content to live — for the time being.

Tapai and Bunmaa were married in a traditional Phu Tai ceremony early in the monsoon season of her seventeenth year. As tradition dictated, she moved in with her husband's extended family who lived not far from her parents. There she stayed with them in a large wooden house built on stilts and with a peaked grass roof. Again, she was the youngest family member and was expected to shoulder the brunt of the daily workload. Tapai's tough and persistent temperament meant that she never shied away from hard work. But Bunmaa was a carefree, fun-loving man who liked to chat while others did the work. He preferred to hire local girls to help plant and harvest his rice crops, often amusing himself by playfully flirting with them while his wife labored nearby — even gossiping to them about Tapai behind her back. Perhaps he was hoping for a jealous reaction; but she feigned indifference, and kept quiet about his indiscretions.

Tapai found herself immersed in endless work — the work of being alive, the work of food and of shelter, the ceaseless tasks of a young wife. Awake before the sun rose, working quickly in pale candlelight, she kindled lumps of black, charred wood heaped loosely in small earthenware stove, fanning the flames until red-hot embers began to glow. Boiling water fed steam into a cone-shaped basket, which cooked the grains of sticky rice with the intense heat of its vapors. An entire day's supply was cooked at once — enough for three meals for her, her husband and some extra for guests.

Farm animals, many living in the backyard or on the packed earth underneath the house, required feed and water. Water was forever a difficult challenge. Neighbors shared communal wells, located at intervals around the village. There the water was drawn by hand to fill wooden buckets, two at a time, which were carried back to the house, suspended from either end of a wooden pole balanced on one shoulder. The villagers went back and forth, again and again, making many trips to fill the large ceramic storage barrels. It was an exhausting task, but it had to be done. Water was needed for drinking and washing: washing dishes, washing clothes and washing dirt and grime from the body after another long sweltering day.

Village life was inextricably bound to the growing of rice. In turn, rice was dependent on the rains, the annual cycle of rejuvenation. Rain was auspicious; it was celebrated. But, it also meant more work, more strenuous, inescapable labor. Plowing began in early May, when the fallow earth soaked up the first heavy downpours. Pairs of enormous water buffaloes were yoked to cumbersome wooden plows and driven repeatedly to one end of the field and back again to loosen the earth. Then they were driven back and forth yet again to trample the clods into mud. Rice seedlings were sprouted in nursery plots and carefully tended — often with water collected from a stream during dry spells — until the rice shoots were ready for planting. Planting was done in rows by groups of women in a timeless choreography. Bending at the waist, the village women walked backwards through thick cloying mud to place the shoots into ground.

The rainy season transformed the countryside into a moist, green patchwork of intersecting rice fields overhung with skies that were heavy with rain. The surrounding hills grew thick with bamboo, and a scrim of fine drizzle softened the outlines of the lush landscape. Rice shoots stood in jagged rows above the still water in which the fields were submerged. The mornings were quiet and hazy with humid heat; and the evenings crackled with the sound of frogs croaking at the edge of the fields and geese clattering in the ponds.

Each rainy season came with its set of anxieties for Tapai. She worried about too little rain in August, when the southwesterly winds began to subside; and flooding in September, when typhoons pounded the land and the rains came down hard, slashing the countryside in sheets. Roads, made muddy by the rains and churned up by carts and water buffaloes, strained the endurance of man and beast. The rain fell inexorably with heavy downpours followed at times by gentle drizzle. Through it all, the rice grew green and tall.

The rice flowered in mid-October. The fields became a sea of golden tassels, undulating softly in the autumn breeze. Tapai joined the whole family as they crowded into the fields to cut rice stalks at harvest time. With quick downward thrusts family members slashed plants with machetes, piling the sheaves on the empty ground between the rows. For weeks, everyone toiled in the bright sunshine, stooped at the waist, blades rising and falling, as they moved down the rows. The sheaves of rice, laden with seeds, were then laid out on the ground and left to dry in the October sunlight.

Tapai's work was now part of her new family's livelihood. She kept house and worked the fields selflessly without complaint. She endured painstaking weeks, pulling out weeds and shoring up dykes. After the harvest, she camped with her husband near the fields to keep vigil over the new crop — the next year's food supply — and to wait for the grains to dry thoroughly so that threshing could begin. Since threshing and winnowing was woman's work, this meant that Tapai and the other women had to spend more chilly nights sleeping in the open when the day's work was over.

Hour upon hour, the women arched backward and bent forward, straining at their waists as they worked to loosen the grain. Lifting sheaves of rice high into the air with both arms, the women thrashed them repeatedly against the ground until the seeds dislodged from the stems to form piles of loose, coarse grain. The loose grain was then winnowed, using large round trays woven from crisscrossing ribbons of split bamboo. Each heavy tray-full was heaved repeatedly into the air until the wispy chaff scattered with the wind. Dried, threshed and winnowed, the new rice was loaded onto massive wooden carts drawn by a team of water buffaloes and hauled to the village, where it was stored loose in the family's small storage barns.

My senses are continually bombarded: the eye
by forms, the ears by sounds, the nose by aromas,
the tongue by flavors and the body by contact.
All of these things I investigate. In that way, each
of my sense faculties becomes a teacher.

Little Kaew

Tapai did not like this busy world, but she tolerated it. Her one
abiding solace had always been the monastery, the religious ceremo-
nies, the spiritual practices. In this vacuum, she was further restricted
by her husband who felt that a woman's place was in the home and
with her family; not in the outside world, and certainly not in
the spiritual world. Very old beliefs divided Phu Tai culture and
community life into separate spheres: high and low, male and female.
That was part of Tapai's world, too. It was ingrained in her upbring-
ing and not to be violated. Tapai's husband allowed her precious little
personal freedom. That was his prerogative and part of the unspoken
marriage bargain. He forbade her to attend observance days at the
monastery, and limited her spiritual activities to offering food to the
monks in the morning and chanting *parittas* at night. She acquiesced
to his demands. She had no other choice.

Tapai's housework and farm chores became the spiritual practices that shaped her married life. Her days were often long and tedious, but she strove to convert the boredom into concentration. She taught herself to concentrate in the midst of the chaos and confusion of life, reining in her mind and forcing herself to focus right in the middle of feeling anger and resentment. When she felt resentment for her husband, she tried to transform her feeling into love and compassion. When she found herself envious of others, she reflected on the life of a renunciant, and on how Ajaan Mun had promised her that one day she would renounce this world to wear the plain white robes of a nun. Tapai understood intuitively the value of deep spiritual practice; but for the moment, she had to content herself with sanctifying the common practices of daily existence.

Dutifully, she attended to all the chores. Aware all the while that she was not content, Tapai felt the boundaries of her constricted life: the small, tight corners of her marriage that hemmed her in on all sides. What she saw, what she heard, what she felt was dissatisfaction. She was seventeen, and before long, she was twenty-seven. It seemed as though every year was a repetition of the same tedium, the same suffering. She resigned herself to things as they were, as they always had been, withdrawing to her contemplative practices, and trying to make the little things sacred.

Tapai began to think more and more about leaving the world behind to don the simple dress and assume the uncomplicated life of a Buddhist nun. Gradually, very quietly, her determination grew, gaining momentum with each passing season until it seemed as though she had never wanted anything else. Finally, one evening after dinner, she knelt beside her husband and tried to make him understand how she felt, how she wanted to be relieved of her domestic duties so she could renounce the world and ordain. Her husband's response was cold and uncompromising. He flatly refused, rejecting all further discussion. Silently, with eyes dutifully cast down, Tapai accepted his judgment and went on with her life.

Tapai's life continued much the same, day after day. Patiently, hopefully, she bided her time. Some weeks later, when she saw her husband in a good mood, she tried again, pleading for her freedom. And again, her husband refused. He said that if he let her become a nun, people would gossip, saying that she left him because he was an unworthy husband, because he'd failed to give her a child.

Tapai didn't know what to say. It was true that they had lived together for ten years without children. They were both surrounded by large, extensive families, but their own family never grew. Perhaps it was a fortunate karmic consequence: this turn of fate should have made it easier for her to simply walk away. Instead, it was used as a reason to thwart her departure. She tried one more time to reason with him, to reach a mutual understanding; but to no avail. His answer was no.

Phu Tai families were generally large. Each birth was celebrated as a victory to their survival, with each new child expected to help bear the workload. Children grew up to share the burden of farming and housekeeping, and then to take care of their parents in old age. After so many years of childless marriage, Tapai's aunts and cousins worried about her welfare: who would look after her when she grew old?

So when one of her cousins — a woman with many children — became pregnant yet again, it was decided that the baby should be given to Tapai to bring up as her own. By prior arrangement with the mother, Tapai helped deliver a healthy baby girl, whom she cradled in her arms and lovingly carried home immediately after birth. Tapai quickly named the girl, "Kaew", her "little darling".

When people noticed Tapai's delight with the baby, and how motherly her affections were, always attentive and caring, they began to call her Mae Kaew, "Kaew's mother". Because it sounded so natural, the name stuck; and from then on, she was known affectionately as Mae Kaew.

Little Kaew grew up to be a spirited and intelligent girl who enthusiastically learned her mother's daily tasks, skillfully imitating Mae Kaew's agile movements and training her young body to assume the rhythm of work until it became second nature. Mae Kaew had been forced by the untimely death of her own mother to develop these skills at a tender age, so she expected her daughter to cultivate the same sense of purpose and commitment.

Raising a daughter became a playful and joyous experience. It distracted Mae Kaew from the confining restrictions of her life, and freed her, at least temporarily, from their tedium. She yearned to share her spiritual longings with someone, but Kaew was still too young, too innocent, too carefree to notice the suffering in the world around her. For Mae Kaew, who had long ago become intimate with the pain and suffering of the world, the affliction borne by those around her affected her like a wound in the chest, sharp and heavy. She felt the harsh unforgiving life of ordinary village people who struggled daily with work. They worked all their lives, from youth through old age, until death. The joy of birth was followed by the sorrow of death; ravaging floods followed by devastating droughts.

The same year that she adopted Kaew, Mae Kaew's father died. Sorrow followed joy. Then, the rains failed, and so did their rice crop. Happiness and suffering, seeming to appear always as a pair, like two wheels of a cart working in tandem to drive a person's life towards death — and future birth, when the wheels started churning anew. Mae Kaew saw that change and suffering were central in life; that everything changed, and no one escaped suffering.

Through the joys and sorrows, the good seasons and the bad, Mae Kaew never relinquished her heart's true aspiration. Being fixed and deeply rooted, below the shifting surface of appearances, renunciation remained the abiding purpose of her existence. She often visualized herself joining the nuns at Wat Nong Nong, shaving her head, wearing plain white garments, living in bare, uncomplicated silence — and meditating again, undisturbed. Renunciation as a way of life. For so many years she had trained herself to live in the world, and not get lost in it; to know the turbulence of her mind and make it peaceful. Happiness and suffering, gladness and sorrow, these were the fluctuations that gave her no peace, the moods that deceived the mind and made her forget herself and her purpose. As she assumed more responsibility with age, peace was losing out to frustration — the nagging disappointment of unfulfillment. Ajaan Mun's parting promise, that one day she would experience the realization of that dream, had always been a sanctuary for her restive heart. But now, with a daughter to bring up, the possibility of ordaining seemed more remote than ever.

Still, if a life of total renunciation was out of the question, perhaps a short retreat could be managed. After all, young village men often ordained temporarily, becoming monks for the duration of a single rains retreat, before returning, reinvigorated, to lay life. It was considered a rite of passage. Even married men renounced the world for short spells. Why couldn't she do the same? Of course, she had her daughter to consider. But at eight years of age, Kaew was already competent enough to do the housework and attend to her father's needs for three months. Mae Kaew could count on her cousins to help out too. To be sure, she would see that all the heavy work was completed first: the backbreaking labor of plowing and planting the rice crop. And she would return home from retreat just in time to bring in the harvest. Her husband had always made it clear that he would never release her to tread the spiritual path. But maybe, with careful planning, an arrangement could be worked out, a compromise of sorts. A little freedom seemed better than no freedom at all; a few steps along the path better than no journey at all.

So again Mae Kaew knelt beside her husband, as she had first done ten years before, and spoke from the heart about her desire to open one small window of freedom in her life, one brief chapter that would be all her own. Her place was the home and the family, she accepted that; but she begged for this short opportunity to realize her lifelong dream. She detailed the arrangements she intended to make, the care she would take to assure that home life ran smoothly in her absence. And she solemnly promised to return as soon as the three-month retreat ended.

Expressionless, staring straight ahead, her husband listened silently until she finished speaking. He then turned to face her, already shaking his head, and, with a dismissive gesture, told her to forget about ordaining. She had a husband to look after and a daughter to raise — and that was a fulltime job. He didn't want to hear anymore about her dreams.

So Mae Kaew crawled back into the tight corners of her life and waited. Patience was a virtue. Compassion and forgiveness were also virtues. She resisted resenting her husband and the restrictions he placed on her. She loved her daughter, and she respected his wishes. But, she did not give up dreaming. Hope, for Mae Kaew, became a saving virtue. So, the following year, with the retreat period approaching, she tried yet again to negotiate a concession from her husband. Though her husband's reply was more conciliatory this time, and less blunt, it was no less dismissive than before, and no less disheartening.

Her predicament was known and gossiped about on both sides of the family. Some were in favor, others opposed. An elderly uncle, respected and admired by all for his wisdom and sense of fairness, was asked to mediate. He had known Mae Kaew since she was a young girl accompanying her father to visit Ajaan Mun, and he sympathized with her righteous intentions. He decided to honor her recently deceased father by arguing for a favorable outcome. Speaking privately with his niece's husband, he extolled the virtues of religious practice and urged him to be fair and reasonable, gently pressuring him to accept a short-term compromise. In the end, an agreement was reached: Bunmaa would allow his wife to ordain for the three-month rains retreat — but not a day longer. As his part of the bargain, he vowed to uphold the integrity of the family and take care of their daughter in her absence. He was even persuaded to observe three months of abstinence, by keeping faith with the five moral precepts until her return: to refrain from killing, stealing, lying, adultery and intoxicants. It was a common, basic religious practice, but one which he rarely had the inclination to follow.

Surprised, bemused and delighted by the sudden turn of events, Mae Kaew raised joined palms to her forehead and let the thankfulness sink in. Ajaan Mun's twenty-year-old prediction was finally coming true. Focusing inward for a moment, she vowed a solemn determination to make the most of her time as a nun. Meditation was foremost in her thoughts, an unfulfilled mission suspended in time, awaiting, and now demanding attention. After so many past disappointments, she would not disappoint herself.

Part Two
Renunciation

Basic training is like a forked stick propping up
a banana tree, which allows a heavy bunch of
bananas to mature and ripen at the right moment
without falling prematurely to the ground.

Leaving It All Behind

On a clear and cloudless Asāḷha full moon day in July, at the age of
thirty-six, Mae Kaew knelt before the monks and nuns at Wat Nong
Nong and, without regret, left behind everything that embodied her
former life, everything that she considered herself to be. By taking
part in an age-old ritual of grace and simplicity, she declared herself
to be a *mae chee*, a rightfully ordained Buddhist nun.

Mae Kaew arrived at the monastery in the early morning to start
her initiation. She greeted the resident nuns with a nervous smile and
sat respectfully to one side, joining them for an austere meal. Finally,
Mae Kaew's long awaited dream of living a life of noble equanimity
and detachment was being realized. One by one, the distinguishing
marks of her old identity were stripped away. Soon she was squatting
anxiously at the well, with butterflies fluttering in her stomach, her
neck extended forward as the head nun, Mae Chee Dang, deftly ma-
neuvered a pair of blunt scissors across her head, chopping off lumps

of long black hair until only a bristly, uneven stubble remained. As hair piled up around her feet, Mae Kaew stared down dispassionately and reflected on the illusory nature of the human body: Hair is not me; it is not mine. Hair, like the rest of the body, is merely a part of nature, a part of the natural physical universe. It belongs to the world, not to me. It is not in any way essential to who I am.

With a finely-tapered razor, honed to precision by constant use, Mae Chee Dang methodically shaved off swaths of dark stubble, revealing the glistening skin of Mae Kaew's scalp and the domed curvature of her skull. Mae Kaew ran the palm of her hand over the smooth surface of her scalp, smiling, letting go.

The other nuns busily gathered around and dressed her in the traditional bleached-white robes of a *mae chee:* a wrap-around skirt that hung freely at the shins, a loose-fitting, long-sleeve blouse buttoned at the neck and a flowing length of cloth that tucked under the right armpit and draped neatly over the left shoulder, a characteristic Buddhist gesture of reverence.

Mae Kaew prostrated three times before Ajaan Khamphan, the senior monk who presided over her ordination. Clasping candles, incense and a lotus flower in her joined palms, she took the Lord Buddha as her refuge: *Buddhaṁ saraṇaṁ gacchāmi...* She took the Dhamma, the transcendent essence of the Buddha's teaching, as her refuge: *Dhammaṁ saraṇaṁ gacchāmi...* And she took the Sangha, the community of noble monks and nuns, as her refuge: *Sanghaṁ saraṇaṁ gacchāmi...* Then, after establishing a serious and thorough resolve to fully commit herself to the training rules, she formally recited the basic precepts of a *mae chee* in front of the entire assembly. She vowed to refrain from harming living creatures; taking what is not given; all sexual conduct; false speech; taking intoxicants; eating after midday; partaking in entertainment and using cosmetics; and using high beds and luxurious seats.

When Mae Kaew finished intoning the training rules, Ajaan Khamphan looked directly at her and advised her to listen carefully while he explained each guiding precept in detail.

For all Buddhists, taking refuge in the Buddha, Dhamma and Sangha is the first and most elemental act on the Buddha's path to freedom. The Buddha is the ideal of spiritual perfection, and the teacher of the true path to attain it. By taking refuge in the Buddha, you take that ideal as your teacher. You also pledge not to seek false spiritual ideals. The Dhamma is the true path to spiritual perfection, and the essence of that perfect truth. By taking refuge in the Dhamma, you take that truth as your goal. You also pledge to avoid wayward paths and false teachings. The Sangha is the embodiment of that essential truth in those who walk the path to attain spiritual perfection. By taking refuge in the Sangha, you take the Buddhist community as your safeguard. You also pledge to avoid the company of fools and wrongdoers. In this way, taking refuge in the Triple Gem of Buddha, Dhamma and Sangha involves a commitment to proper spiritual ideals, as well as a fundamental sense of restraint.

The Triple refuge is the foundation to genuine freedom. The training rules create the conditions and set the parameters for walking the path that leads to liberation. Maintaining them religiously frees the mind from guilt and remorse, and has a strong protective quality, warding off danger. To begin with, you must never kill another living creature, no matter how small; nor should you incite others to kill or oppress. Every living being values its life, so you must not destroy that intrinsic value by putting an end to the very life that a being holds dear. Instead, let compassion for all living creatures fill your heart.

You should never steal another's possessions, or encourage others to do so. All beings cherish their possessions. Even things that do not appear to have much value, are nonetheless valued by their owner. Therefore nothing belonging to another person should be debased by theft. Such actions debase not only the possessions, but people's hearts as well. So let charity and openness be your guiding principles.

From now on, you must abstain from all sexual relations, leading an entirely celibate life. Sexual energy and the passions it arouses destroy tranquility of body and mind and run counter to the goal of the spiritual life. Let the energy of pure love and devotion arise in its place.

You must abstain from lying, and always tell the truth. Never be dishonest or deceitful, in your speech or actions. Lies undermine trust and cause people to lose all respect for each other. Let the power of truth free your mind.

The final four precepts represent principles of spiritual training that help create the conditions for a calm body and a clear mind. To that end, you must never consume alcoholic beverages, or any form of intoxicant that muddles the mind and impairs good judgment. Solid food must not be eaten after midday. You must abstain from singing, dancing and other forms of entertainment, and not adorn yourself with jewelry and flowers, or beautify yourself with perfume and cosmetics. You must avoid sleeping on high beds with soft mattresses, or sitting on ornately decorated seats with soft cushions.

By conscientiously observing these eight precepts, you temporarily close the door on the household life, and open a window onto the path of liberation. Keep in mind that the real purpose of observing them is to embody their basic principles in all you think, say and do. In that way, you can train the mind to sever the fetters that bind you to the cycle of repeated birth and death.

Practicing the precepts not only puts a stop to evil, but also promotes the cultivation of all that is good. By restraining the mind and shutting the door on harmful behavior that leads to pain and suffering, and by promoting the purity of mind and action that leads to liberation, these training rules provide the essential foundation for all Buddhist practice. As such, they form the basis for all monastic discipline. Always remember that the training rules are part of the path to spiritual liberation, so practice them diligently, with the dignity and respect they deserve.

Having inspired the candidate and motivated her with a sense of purpose, Ajaan Khamphan chanted a formal blessing to sanctify the occasion and confirm her new status as a fully ordained *mae chee*. With that, Mae Chee Kaew had finally fulfilled her lifelong ambition.

I've endured many hardships to test my determination. I went without food for many days. I
refused to lie down to sleep for many nights.
Endurance became the food to nourish my heart
and diligence the pillow to rest my head.

Reclaiming Lost Treasure

Mae Chee Kaew withdrew from the world and entered a cloistered
spiritual realm. Although her dream was achieved, her work had just
begun. The nuns lived in their own section of the monastery, separated from the monks' quarters by tall, thick clumps of tangled bamboo.
Here Mae Chee Kaew was given a tiny hut, so newly constructed that
its split bamboo floor and walls were still freshly green and shiny, and
the thatch of its grass roof still dense and bushy.

Mae Chee Dang was the senior-most nun in the community. Mae
Chee Kaew had been present six years earlier when Mae Chee Dang
solemnly took her vows in this same monastery, and had always
admired and respected her, both as a close family friend and as a
devout and dedicated renunciant. She set the example for the younger
nuns who looked to her for inspiration. Together with Mae Chee
Ying, who ordained shortly after her, Mae Chee Dang made sure that

the small group of women at Wat Nong Nong remained focused and in proper harmony.

Mae Chee Kaew began her new life by stepping into its quiet rhythm at the earliest stirring of the first new day. She rose at three a.m. each morning and washed the sleep from her face with handfuls of cold water. She then lit a candle lantern and stepped onto the meditation path beside her hut to take up her practice. Silently repeating 'bud...dho, bud...dho' with each pair of footsteps, she internalized her senses and concentrated her mind until she felt fully awake and sufficiently fresh to continue her meditation in a seated position. Sitting still and erect, she maintained her calm, peaceful concentration until daybreak. She then hurried toward the main *sala* to join the monks and nuns for the morning chanting.

When the soft cadence of the chanting faded to a close, the monks and nuns remained in a still, contemplative silence for several minutes. Afterwards, the nuns gathered in the open-air kitchen to cook rice and prepare simple dishes to augment the offerings the monks received on their daily alms round. Mae Chee Kaew cheerfully helped with the cooking chores and then joined the nuns for their daily meal. Like the monks, the nuns ate only one meal a day, a practice that suited their meditative lifestyle. Eating less often, and only small amounts, lightens the work of meditation: eating too much can easily make the mental faculties sluggish and unresponsive, and greed and obsession for food can be a corrosive poison in the mind. Once the chores of cooking and cleaning were completed, the nuns turned their full attention to meditation, buoyant in body and spirit, and free of concern about food for the rest of the day.

Taking care of simple necessities, such as cooking and cleaning, the nuns helped foster the well-being of the whole monastic community. Mindful and composed, each afternoon they emerged from their dwellings to pick up long-handled brooms of flexible bamboo twigs, and swept clean the area around each hut and the winding paths that interlaced the nuns' quarters. They then dusted and swept the kitchen area, put the pots and dishes neatly away and remembered to place handfuls of raw rice in water to soak overnight. They bathed and laundered quietly at the well. In the gathering dusk, the nuns walked together to the main *sala* to join the monks for the evening chanting. Because it was dark by the time the meeting adjourned, the nuns used long-stem candles to guide them back to their dwellings, where they continued to meditate late into the night.

Striving alone at her small hut, Mae Chee Kaew alternated between walking and sitting as she struggled to regain her former adeptness at deep concentration. She had not practiced formal meditation since Ajaan Mun left her village twenty years before, and the rigors of her personal life and household cluttered her mind with endless petty concerns. Still, it had also taught her the value of effort. So, she fixed her mind and worked on her meditation as if it were a rice field, stolidly plowing it through, furrow upon furrow, *buddho* upon *buddho*.

She had always known how to work with persistence and perseverance. These were qualities she could count on. Once she put her worldly life firmly behind, narrowing her focus on the bare simplicity of the task at hand, she progressed swiftly on a path that would frighten most people in their first few steps. Seated in meditation, surrounded by the late-night stillness, her body and mind seemed to fall abruptly, as if off a steep cliff, or down a well; and everything

vanished into absolute stillness. Nothing registered in her awareness
but the awareness itself — awareness permeated with a knowing presence so profound and so vibrant that it totally transcended body
and mind. The experience lasted for only a brief moment, a moment
of perfect peace. As she emerged from it, her mind sharp and radiant-
ly clear, she knew that she had finally reclaimed a lost treasure.

Emerging gradually from that state of deep samādhi, she felt a
strange and unfamiliar vista open within her heart, as though she had
awakened in the midst of a dream. Seemingly out of nowhere, the
ghost-like image of a man, his head severed at the trunk, floated slowly into her vision. Watching with horror, Mae Chee Kaew saw that
the headless ghost had a single fiery eyeball embedded in the middle
of its chest, a red-hot orb that stared directly at her with menacing
ferocity. Feeling threatened, and unprepared, she thought to escape.
As her concentration wavered, her fear and uncertainty increased. In
concert with her mounting fear, the ghastly apparition grew in size
and intensity, as though feeding off the fear's negative energy. Panic
began to envelop her heart. Then suddenly, she remembered Ajaan
Mun and his advice to never run away from fear, but to always face
it with mindfulness and clear comprehension. With that reminder, a
clear awareness reasserted itself, fixing her mind firmly again in the
present moment, a moment of pure and simple perception. Focusing
on the intense feeling of panic pulsating in her heart, and withdrawing
her attention from the headless ghost, allowed her emotional state to
stabilize and the fear to gradually subside and disappear. And with
that, the frightening vision simply faded away and vanished.

Withdrawing from samādhi and returning to ordinary conscious
ness, Mae Chee Kaew contemplated the dangers presented by fear.

She realized intuitively that the fear itself was the real danger, not the image that induced it. Images perceived in meditation are merely mental phenomena that have no inherent power to harm one's body or mind. They are neutral, and, in and of themselves, carry no specific meaning. The mind's interpretation of them is the crucial point, and the source of danger. An interpretation brings about a reaction of fear and loathing, which are poisonous and negative emotions that destabilize the mind, threaten its equilibrium and endanger its sanity. Focusing attention on the terrifying aspects of an image instinctively magnifies the negative emotional reaction, and increases the danger. Withdrawing attention from the image, and focusing on the fear itself, restores it solidly to the present moment, where fear and image can no longer co-exist. Mae Chee Kaew realized then, with clear insight, that only unrestrained fear could harm her in meditation.

The meditation that Ajaan Mun had taught her was deceptively simple, and the rhythmic repetition of *buddho* made it appear easy. But the massive effort required to focus her mind on a single object after so many years of neglect made meditation frustratingly difficult at first. She felt her body and mind out of sync, as though they were tugging against each other. The mind needed one thing, the body wanted another; the mind wanted this, the body needed that. Disharmony prevailed. Too much food brought lethargy; too little escalated errant thinking. She pondered how to balance eating and sleeping, walking and sitting, communal and personal. She wondered how to maintain a sharp, mindful focus during each changing moment, and every new circumstance, throughout the day.

Mae Chee Kaew experimented with fasting, going entirely without food for several days at a time. But she discovered that lack of food left her feeling mentally dull and sluggish, and vulnerable to changing moods and wayward thoughts, as if the flow of her spiritual energy was somehow constricted. That subtle hindrance seemed to lessen her motivation to intensify in meditation. She knew that many of the monks in Ajaan Mun's tutelage found fasting to be a valuable tool for advancing their spiritual development. They regularly endured hunger and discomfort because fasting increased their mental vigilance, making the mind bold, and its focus sharp. But Mae Chee Kaew's mind failed to respond positively. So in the end, she concluded that going without food did not suit her temperament.

Going without sleep, however, was a different matter. Mae Chee Kaew passed most of the second month of her retreat in three postures: sitting, standing and walking, but never lying down. She started the "sitter's practice" as another experiment, an attempt to find a practical way of accelerating her meditation that took advantage of her natural strengths. She discovered that refraining from sleep rendered her mind so bright and sharp, so calm and serene, mindful and alert, that she practiced continuously for twenty-one days without ever lying down.

With each day of sleeplessness, her meditation deepened and her confidence grew. Sharpened spiritual faculties made her courageous and daring, which coordinated perfectly with her bold and adventurous nature. Her unusual visions, more frequent than before, became more extraordinary as well: sometimes foreseeing future events or perceiving nonphysical realms; at times revealing profound truths of the Buddha's teaching.

Emerging from deep samādhi late one night, Mae Chee Kaew saw a vision of her body lifeless and stretched across a weaver's loom.

Consumed by an advanced state of decay, the body was bloated and discolored, and the skin had split open, oozing pus. Writhing maggots, sleek and fat, were devouring the rotting flesh. The graphic realness of the vision shocked and frightened her. Suddenly she felt Ajaan Mun's presence close behind her, as though he were peering over her shoulder at the grotesque scene. Slowly, deliberately, he reminded her that death is the natural consequence of birth — all creatures born into this world will eventually die, their bodies decaying and returning to their natural elements in precisely the same manner. Indeed, everything in the universe is impermanent and constantly changing. Everything will disintegrate and disappear. Although death is always with us, we rarely contemplate it. Ajaan Mun then instructed her that she must start to earnestly contemplate her own birth, ageing, sickness and death.

Be a nun in the truest sense. You don't want to spoil your vocation by mingling with the foul-smelling grit of worldly life, so don't glance back, longing for your home and family.

Stirring up a Hornet's Nest

Little Kaew spent the rainy months working around the house and playing with her cousins. She was a happy, cheerful girl, but she missed her mother's calm and comforting presence. She worked hard to please her father, Bunmaa, but he often appeared distracted by some inner turmoil. He frequently left home in the morning, and did not return until late at night.

On lunar observance days, Kaew followed the womenfolk to Wat Nong Nong and joined her mother for daily chores, chatting incessantly about life at home. What she said worried Mae Chee Kaew: her husband's regular disappearances were unusual, and, from what Kaew described, he seemed to be intoxicated when he returned. Mae Chee Kaew decided, for her daughter's sake, that she should visit home occasionally to help with the housework and to keep an eye on the situation.

Entering the house, her husband's absence was the first thing she noticed. Mae Chee Kaew spent whole days cleaning, laundering and cooking for her daughter, but Bunmaa never appeared. During the last month of her retreat, Mae Chee Kaew went home once a week, but she never once caught sight of him. Rumors soon reached her that he was secretly having an affair with a woman from another village, a young widow with two children. She was told that he had started drinking and carousing in her absence.

Mae Chee Kaew was repelled by her husband's behavior. Now weary of her marriage and wishing to make the noble path her life, the thought of returning home was unbearable to her. While Mae Chee Kaew was morally obliged to keep her word, her husband's failure to adhere to the fundamental rules of moral conduct jeopardized the future of their marriage.

As the retreat approached its final days, Mae Chee Kaew agonized over her next course of action. She felt no desire to return to married life, but she was deeply concerned about the well-being of her daughter. She wanted to remain close to Kaew, to guide and comfort her; but at ten years of age, Kaew was still too young to live at the monastery with her mother. Besides, having renounced all worldly possessions, she had no means to support a child, but only the meager daily rations sufficient to sustain one person.

Slowly, following several weeks of deliberation, the idea took shape in Mae Chee Kaew's mind that she could combine both the household and the monastic worlds into her daily life. By spending her daylight hours at home being a mother and a wife, she could fulfill her worldly obligations; by passing her nights at the monastery, absorbed in meditation, she could pursue her spiritual goals. As un-

orthodox and unrealistic as the scheme seemed, she was willing —
even desperate — to try it.

So, as agreed, Mae Chee Kaew returned home on the final day of
the rains retreat. However, she had not relinquished her white robes.
Nor had she given up her vows. She remained an ordained *mae chee*,
but wore a black skirt and blouse over her white robes, to disguise
her true intentions. She spent the morning and afternoon with Kaew,
completing the day's housework, and cooking the evening meal. She
planned to serve her family dinner, and then quickly return to the
monastery before dusk. When Kaew and Bunmaa sat down to eat,
she served the food but refrained from eating as she continued to
observe the nun's training rule to forego meals after midday. Mae
Chee Kaew's abstinence provoked her husband's anger. He demanded
the reason for her behavior, and commanded her to sit and eat. When
she refused, he leapt from his seat and tried to grab her by the arm.
Mae Chee Kaew jumped away, racing down the steps and away from
the house. Bunmaa started to give chase but was quickly restrained by
Mae Chee Kaew's older brother, P'In. He advised Bunmaa to let her
go. Furious, Bunmaa bellowed that their marriage was finished. He
yelled after her that if she wanted any part of their possessions, she
could sue him in the provincial high court. As Mae Chee Kaew ran
through the village in the descending twilight, she felt drained by the
pain and suffering of her worldly life and at that moment decided
to never disrobe.

Mae Chee Kaew arrived back at the monastery to find that everyone was worried about her. When she recounted what took place, the
senior-most nun, Mae Chee Dang, scolded her: "Why bother going
back to your husband? You're just stirring up a hornet's nest. Take a

lesson and stop sticking your hand into the fire. Even if you don't get burned, your reputation will be."

Mae Chee Kaew debated cutting off all contact with her husband. But her brothers urged her to settle her affairs with him first. Heeding their advice, she returned to the house several days later to negotiate a formal settlement to their marriage. Her husband was in no mood to compromise. He insisted that everything she had acquired since their marriage rightfully belonged to him. All that remained to decide was what to do with the belongings she had inherited from her parents. Having already renounced the world and its material possessions, Mae Chee Kaew found it natural, even gratifying, to give everything she owned to Bunmaa and ask for nothing, except this: that she be allowed to keep the small knife she had always used to cut betel nut. Her husband quickly retorted that she had acquired the knife during their marriage, and it was therefore his. With that final dismissal, Mae Chee Kaew completely turned her back to domestic life and relinquished all worldly possessions, without exception.

Having finalized the agreement, Mae Chee Kaew spoke privately with her daughter. Carefully and in detail, she told little Kaew about the events reshaping their lives, and asked for her patience and understanding. Learning of her mother's intention to leave home for good, little Kaew pleaded with a childish innocence for the chance to accompany her mother and live with her at the monastery. With a heart heavy with sympathy, Mae Chee Kaew described the austere conditions of a nun's life. She explained that since she had now given everything to her father, she had no means to adequately support her daughter. Besides, the monastery wasn't a place to bring up a child.

Gently, but insistently, Mae Chee Kaew urged the child to remain with her father for the time being. She explained that Kaew's father had the resources to look after her needs, and reassured Kaew that his wealth and property would be her rightful inheritance. When Kaew reached maturity, she could, if she still wished, live with her mother. Mae Chee Kaew would welcome her with an open heart and be her spiritual guide and companion for life. Reluctantly, but obediently, Kaew finally accepted her mother's urging to remain with her father.

Mae Chee Kaew walked back to the monastery in a quiet and pensive mood, replaying the pros and cons of her decision to permanently separate from her family and friends. In the end, her thoughts always came to rest with Prince Siddhartha, who left his wife and son and princely inheritance behind to follow the spiritual path, unencumbered by worldly concerns. Although he abandoned universally honored parental obligations, he did so for the sake of the supremely noble goal of unconditional awakening to the truth of Dhamma, and the total destruction of the cycle of birth and death. Becoming a fully enlightened being, the Lord Buddha's achievement transcended all mundane sacrifices, and all worldly conventions. Having freed himself from suffering, he had helped countless living beings do the same. With the ultimate goal of the holy life clearly and unalterably fixed in her mind, Mae Chee Kaew was inspired to follow steadfastly in the Buddha's footsteps.

Carefully observe the ebb and flow of defiling influences in your mind. Don't let them deceive you so readily. When you're skilled enough to catch their movements, you can transform their negative power into positive spiritual energy.

Simply Fetching Water

$\mathscr{M}$ae Chee Kaew's bold move created a stir of excitement in Baan Huay Sai's close-knit community. Interested parties on both sides of the family voiced strong opinions. Being local women themselves, the nuns at Wat Nong Nong could not avoid becoming caught up in the ongoing drama. They supported Mae Chee Kaew in her decision – most of them had even encouraged it. But the situation attracted unwanted attention to their community, which led to the involvement of village affairs in monastic life. This unwelcome intrusion was further exacerbated by the close proximity of the monastery to the village. A reasonable solution was therefore urgently needed to protect spiritual harmony from being disrupted by mundane village concerns. Changing locations started to become a serious possibility as the nuns considered ways to distance themselves. Mae Chee Dang was convinced that the religious community, for the sake of its long-term well-being, must move far enough away that village affairs could no longer impinge daily upon its tranquil environment.

Ajaan Khamphan, the abbot of Wat Nong Nong monastery, was a longtime disciple of Ajaan Sao Kantasīlo, and a *dhutanga* monk well respected for his strict discipline and proficiency in meditation. As abbot of the monastery and spiritual guide to his disciples, Ajaan Khamphan assumed responsibility for the community's welfare. Because the monks were also adversely affected by local events, Mae Chee Dang and Mae Chee Ying discussed the matter at length with Ajaan Khamphan. Ultimately, the decision would be his. After close consultation with the monks and nuns, he chose to move to a nearby mountain range along with those who wished to accompany him and establish a new forest monastery.

Phu Gao Mountain was located in a small range of the Phu Phan foothills, six miles northwest of Baan Huay Sai. In an age of foot trails and buffalo carts, the rugged terrain made it a remote and inaccessible destination for the casual visitor. The upper ridges were covered with solid sandstone cliffs that dropped precipitously twenty or thirty feet to densely forested slopes of tall bamboos and hardwoods. The massive strata of rock that stretched along the cliffs' length were tinted dark brown by the dry lichen clinging to their surface. The cliff jutted out over the slope below, forming natural recesses of long open grottos beneath the overhanging rock to offer protection from the harsh sun and rain. Lacking suitable dwellings at first, the monks and nuns took up residence in these bare, earthy caves, making simple platforms from bamboo, raised on stout legs several feet above the damp ground. There they lived and meditated, each in a separate location. Having no toilets, they relieved themselves at the edge of the cliffs, with an audience of amused monkeys watching from the trees.

Water was a fundamental necessity, and a major concern. The closest reliable supply lay a half hour's walk from the caves in a stream that tumbled through a shallow depression between two ridges. It was decided, by mutual consent, that the junior nuns would be given the task of fetching water for the whole community, while the monks worked with local farmers to build the basic structures needed to lay the foundation for a new monastery.

Each day after the meal, Mae Chee Kaew helped the other nuns perform their water duties. She picked up two empty buckets, hung them from a long, straight bamboo pole and started to walk, descending a steep, narrow path intersected by tree roots and protruding stones, until she reached the stream. She knelt on the bank and watched as the buckets filled with fresh, cool water. Fixing one full bucket to each end of the pole, she centered the load on one shoulder and climbed back up the trail, over roots and around boulders, taking care not to spill her precious cargo. She reached the cave, tired and out of breath; yet prepared for more trips. After emptying the buckets, she returned to the stream for another load, and then again for another.

Fetching water was a tedious job. It called for the same routine each day, trudging down, then up, down, then up... Every day Mae Chee Kaew followed the routine. And her resolve never wavered. Determined to convert mundane adversity into spiritual virtue, she meditated on *buddho* as she walked — silently intoning *bud* with one step, *dho* with the next. As her heart calmed, the buckets felt lighter and the work more effortless. Once her heart had opened, carrying water became a simple task: nothing more or less than what she was doing, here and now, in the present, one mindful step at a time.

Occasionally Mae Chee Kaew's brothers came to visit her at Phu Gao Mountain. They were shocked and dismayed to see her living conditions, and the hardship she endured. They loved their sister and wanted to show solidarity with her cause. So they helped the nuns fetch water from the stream, hauling it up the mountain, two heavy bucketfuls at a time. But no amount of collected water was enough to satisfy the needs of six monks and five nuns. In the end, tired and dispirited, her brothers tried to persuade her to return with them to Baan Huay Sai, where they could properly look after her needs. They assured her that her husband had remarried, sold their house and moved with Kaew and his new family to a distant province. But Mae Chee Kaew was steadfast in her determination to remain with Ajaan Khamphan and pursue an austere, meditative lifestyle on Phu Gao Mountain.

As time went on, and the mountain monastery began to take shape, water shortage became an obstacle that seemed to threaten its long-term survival. All attempts to discover a nearby source had failed. One evening, out of desperation, Mae Chee Kaew sat down, crossed her legs, straightened her back and focused inward. She made the solemn resolve that if she and the others were destined to stay at Phu Gao Mountain, she would discover a convenient source. She then practiced her meditation as usual. Later that night, as her mind withdrew from deep samādhi, a vision spontaneously surfaced of eleven pools of water, overgrown with vines and tall grasses. She recognized the mountainous terrain, for she had walked past the area several times and it was only a short distance from the main cave.

At Mae Chee Kaew's urging, the nuns searched the area the following day. As Mae Chee Kaew indicated, they found many pools of water beneath the thick vegetation. Delighted, Ajaan Khamphan had the nuns and local villagers cut back the vines and grasses and dig sediment out of the pools, some of which were twenty feet deep. When the work was complete, they found enough fresh water to supply the needs of the monks and nuns all year round.

People suffer because they grasp and don't
let go. Dissatisfaction follows them everywhere.
Look carefully at your own heart and learn how
to relinquish the cause of suffering.

Through the Access Gate

While living in the cliffs at Phu Gao Mountain, Mae Chee Kaew
came upon many strange and unusual phenomena in her nightly meditation. They were extraordinary; things that she never experienced
before. As she emerged slightly from deep samādhi, Mae Chee Kaew
found her mind entering a familiar world of intersecting spiritual
energies; a world occupied by countless realms of nonphysical living
beings. Some of these beings hailed from the dark and lowly regions,
where they suffered the consequences of their evil deeds; others came
from the lofty spheres of radiance inhabited by celestial *devas* and
brahmas. It was as though her meditation delivered her to an open gate,
where her heart felt the pull of competing force fields, each vying
for her attention. Ajaan Mun had called it "access concentration",
warning her how vulnerable she was to the disparate spiritual energies that she might encounter there, and how she must establish
steadfast control over her mind before stepping out the gate. While

Mae Chee Kaew took heed of Ajaan Mun's advice, she was curious and venturesome by nature, and could not resist the temptation to venture out and look around.

What she witnessed both fascinated and horrified her. Disembodied spirits called — some howling, others screaming, or weeping — besieging her, begging, pleading for redemption from the miserable retribution of their own misdeeds. Forms and faces clung to them like shrouds, the ghostly remnants of some past existence, some previous life, which followed them like deathly souvenirs from an unfinished journey. All pleaded for her attention, her sympathy, her grace — some gesture that would shine a ray of hope into the darkened corner of their existence.

Often the disembodied spirits of slain animals appeared in her meditative visions, begging for a share of her spiritual merit to help them overcome their immense suffering. Late one night, just after Mae Chee Kaew had withdrawn from samādhi, a disembodied consciousness of a recently slain water buffalo appeared in front of her, wailing in pain and bemoaning its fate. Suspended in her vision, like a ghostly apparition, the buffalo immediately communicated its sad history. As Mae Chee Kaew absorbed the message with her heart, the buffalo related that its owner was a fierce and cruel man whose heart lacked all kindness and compassion. He very often put his buffalo to work, pulling ploughs or wagons from dawn until dusk, and never showed any appreciation for the animal's daily hardship. On top of that, this merciless master beat and tortured the buffalo constantly. In the end, the poor animal was tied to a tree and brutally slaughtered for the sake of its meat. Before dying, it endured unspeakable pain and torment. It bellowed loudly, ripping the air with a sickening

sound as its skull was repeatedly bludgeoned, until it finally collapsed, unconscious. The disembodied consciousness of the buffalo,
still traumatized and clinging to the remnants of its old form, was
hoping for a share of Mae Chee Kaew's merit and virtue so that it
might have the opportunity to be reborn as a human being.

Instinctively sensing Mae Chee Kaew's compassionate nature, the
spirit poured out the collective pain and suffering of its species to her.
The buffalo described the brutality a water buffalo must endure; the
unrelenting mistreatment and neglect by human beings, and constant
abuse from other animals. Even a person, living in abject poverty, does
not have to suffer the torment and indignity that a farm animal does.
For that reason, the buffalo longed to be born as a human being in its
next life.

Mae Chee Kaew was surprised to hear a tale of such cruelty. She
was familiar with many of the local farmers and found them to be
kindhearted and friendly people. Through her samādhi vision, she
conveyed her suspicions to the animal. The buffalo claimed that its
owner was a fierce and cruel man, lacking human decency; but the
buffalo's heart was obviously full of hatred and vengeance, which may
have distorted the truth. Mae Chee Kaew wondered that perhaps the
water buffalo itself was misbehaving. Perhaps the owner beat it for a
good reason. Opening her heart to the spirit, she communicated her
query: "Did you ever eat the vegetables that people planted in their
gardens? Did you chew on the vegetables that people had carefully
planted beside their fields? The farmers who live in this area are
normally kind and gentle people. Why should they torment you if
you did nothing wrong? It seems to me that you must have behaved
badly to receive such treatment. Am I right?"

The reply of the slain water buffalo deeply touched Mae Chee Kaew's heart. It admitted, "I did such things only out of ignorance. I was worked in the fields all day, and was never allowed in the pasture to graze. Hunger and fatigue drove me to eat whatever plants I could forage. All vegetation looked the same to me. It never occurred to me that certain plants might have an owner who was keeping an eye on them. I had no intention to steal. Had I understood human language, I might never have made that mistake. But people are far more intelligent than animals, so they should be more sympathetic and forgiving of our natural habits. They shouldn't just mercilessly exercise their power over other creatures, especially when it violates human standards of moral decency. A good person doesn't behave in such a shameful and offensive manner. Most of the farmers in this area are actually kind and gentle people, like you said. But my former master, Mr. Ton, is a fierce and cruel man who lacks human decency. That scum of the earth is a man so pitiless that he is incapable of sympathy or forgiveness. He's even cruel to his fellow men, to say nothing of lowly animals."

Since childhood, Mae Chee Kaew had always felt a profound compassion for the plight of farm animals. She fed her cows and water buffalo lumps of sticky rice every day, whispering sweetly in their ears that because they worked the rice fields, they too deserved to eat rice. For that reason, the animals were very fond of her, and felt appreciated. For example, when the rope around its neck, holding the cow bell, broke, the cow would walk straight to Mae Chee Kaew to alert her about the lost bell instead of wandering away, undetected and grateful for its freedom. Nonetheless, Mae Chee Kaew realized that even those animals which were well treated by their masters were still bound by their *kamma* to a life of constant suffering.

Mae Chee Kaew knew that feelings of hatred and revenge are major causes of birth in the lower realms of existence. Sensing the anger in her unfortunate visitor, she taught it the dangers inherent in a hate-filled, vengeful state of mind. She warned that those negative emotions ran counter to its desire to be born as a human being in its next life. If it really expected to be born human, it must keep such destructive mental defilements under control.

Mae Chee Kaew explained that the five moral precepts are the basis of a decent human being. If the spirit were to have any chance to be reborn in a human form, it must make a solemn resolve to abide by these fundamental rules of conduct. It must not take life, or cause injury to other creatures; it must not steal, or take things that belong to others, like the vegetables people plant in their gardens; it must not commit adultery, or engage in harmful sexual practices; it must not lie, or deliberately deceive others; and it must not indulge in any substance that causes intoxication or drunkenness.

By killing, stealing, committing adultery and lying, you not only do harm to others, but you also violate the spirit of openness and trust that forms the basis of human relations. Indulging in intoxication is considered evil because it clouds the mind and readily conduces to the other four offences. From a karmic viewpoint, such actions result in rebirth among common animals, hungry ghosts or the hell realms. In these lower realms of existence, suffering is intense, and a weakened capacity for spiritual development makes it very difficult to produce the necessary conditions for rebirth in the higher realms. Therefore, faithfully observing the moral precepts prevents the possibility of being born into the lower realms, and helps to ensure that you will be born as a human being. So, if you can maintain this level of moral virtue, and renounce the tendency to think, speak and act in evil ways, then you can truly expect to be rewarded with a human birth — if not now, then in the future.

Fully sympathetic to the troubled spirit's desperate condition, Mae Chee Kaew compassionately resolved to share with it her spiritual merit and virtue, hoping that might help to sow the seeds of rebirth in the human realm: "May the merit and virtue that I share with you now help to guard your behavior, nourish your spirit and lead you on the path to develop the spiritual qualities needed to gain birth in a realm of real happiness."

Having rejoiced in Mae Chee Kaew's exceptional virtue and received her blessing, the disembodied spirit of the water buffalo departed in a bright, happy, cheerful mood, as though it was off to be reborn in its chosen realm of happiness.

Early the next morning, Mae Chee Kaew called aside one of the local villagers and quietly told him what had happened the night before. She requested him to inquire about Mr. Ton, the water buffalo's former owner, and find out where he lived and what had transpired between him and the buffalo. But she warned the man not to let Mr. Ton know she had asked him to investigate the matter. Feeling disgraced, he might think badly of Mae Chee Kaew, which would merely increase his store of evil *kamma*.

The villager immediately replied that he and Mr. Ton lived in the same village and that he knew the man well. He knew for a fact that Mr. Ton had lashed his water buffalo to a tree and slaughtered it at eight o'clock the previous night. The agonizing cries of the poor animal could be heard throughout the neighborhood. After killing it, the man roasted its meat and held a big party for his friends. They feasted all night, making a great commotion yelling, laughing and carousing until nearly dawn.

Acts of evil always dismayed Mae Chee Kaew. On a deep, personal level, she felt a strong pang of lament and sorrow, as though the transgressor were her own child, whose brutal actions had betrayed her trust in humanity's inherent goodness. She witnessed perpetrator and victim trading places in a karmic dance of blame and revenge, cruelty and hatred, spiraling downward, birth after birth, toward lower and darker realms of existence. Mae Chee Kaew told her supporter that the buffalo's only hope of redemption lay in renouncing hatred and vengeance, and rejoicing in the virtuous deeds of others. Although its ghostly existence prevented it from performing acts of merit, it could still participate in others' good deeds by applauding those acts and spiritually identifying itself with the resulting merit and virtue. By creating a spiritual bond with her, the deceased buffalo had taken a positive step forward to a favorable rebirth.

Beings who still wander through the round of saṁsāra should reflect carefully on these events, for similar circumstances could befall anyone who neglects to promote spiritual virtue, or disdains the practice of fundamental moral principles.

Don't just eat and sleep like a common animal.
Make sure you remain disenchanted with worldly life and have a healthy fear of future birth.
Don't just sit around idly, keeping vigil over the
smoldering embers of your life.

The Wild Boar

Mae Chee Kaew communicated with nonphysical beings using
the nonverbal language of the heart, the common language shared
by all sentient beings. A nonphysical being's flow of consciousness
infuses thoughts and emotions with meaning and intent — just as
the style and content of verbal expressions are determined by the flow
of human consciousness. Each current of thought that issues from a
conscious flow is attuned to a specific meaning and purpose, and thus
communicates a clear and unmistakable message. When a thought
current intersects with the knowing quality of another conscious flow,
it imparts a message directly to the receiving consciousness, as a fully
formed and coherent idea or opinion. Using direct nonverbal dialogue,
Mae Chee Kaew questioned her nonphysical visitors, inquiring about
their histories and listening to their stories. She wanted to help them;
but, mostly, all she could do was share with them the merit of her

meditation and the purity of her spiritual life. It was for them to receive and make use of these merits as best they could.

An even more bizarre incident than her communication with the water buffalo occurred when the disembodied consciousness of a slain wild boar appeared as a samādhi image in Mae Chee Kaew's meditation. Wandering alone at night in search of food on the far side of Phu Gao Mountain, the boar was killed by a local hunter, who hid near a watering hole frequented by wild animals, waiting for his next kill.

In the early hours before dawn, a ghostly image of the wild boar arose spontaneously in Mae Chee Kaew's visual field. Accustomed to seeing such apparitions, she directed the flow of her consciousness, immediately asking the boar's reason for coming to see her. The boar spoke haltingly, stammering as though still in a state of shock. The boar explained that it was killed on its way to the watering hole by a hunter, named Dum. Mae Chee Kaew wondered why the boar had not been more cautious about being shot. The wild boar pleaded with her to understand that it had always been extremely wary of hunters, always on guard as its very life depended on it. But a wild animal's existence was unimaginably difficult, and its suffering, unbearably harsh. Living in the wild, totally at the mercy of nature's shifting seasons, boars lived in constant fear. Their lives were constantly in danger, threatened by natural predators, as well as hunters and trappers. By being extremely vigilant, the boar had survived many years in the mountains; but, in the end, it could not avoid being killed.

The wild boar told Mae Chee Kaew that it was terrified of being reborn as a wild animal, enduring a life of unbelievable pain and suffering, a life of persistent fear and distrust. A boar could never relax nor find peace. Fearful that it could not avoid another animal birth, the boar came to Mae Chee Kaew to beg for a share of her spiritual merit and virtue to boost its chances of being reborn as a human being. Miserably, the spirit told her that it lacked a sufficient store of merit and virtue to be confident about its future state. The boar had nothing of value to offer her — except the meat from its freshly-killed body. Thus it implored her to kindly eat some of its meat so that she might gain the bodily strength required to maintain her exemplary spiritual lifestyle. At the same time, this would allow the boar to make merit.

Eagerly, the wild boar informed Mae Chee Kaew that, the next morning, the hunter's family would bring meat from its carcass as an offering to the monastery. The boar begged her to eat it, hoping that this act of generosity would bring enough merit for it to be reborn as a human being. The boar wished to offer her the choicest cuts of meat from its body; however, people are greedy by nature, so it feared the hunter's family would keep the best parts for themselves and leave only the lower quality meat as its offering to Mae Chee Kaew.

Mae Chee Kaew was fascinated by her visitor's request. In many years of meditation, she had never come across an instance where the consciousness of a dead animal attempted to make merit by offering the meat from its own body. Feeling profound sympathy for its hapless plight, while radiating loving kindness, she silently acknowledged the charitable intention. She inspired the wild boar with the virtues of generosity, instilling a feeling of pride in doing good deeds. As with so many beings of the lower realms, she emphasized the benefits of the five moral precepts as the basis of a human birth, and encouraged the boar to adopt them as training rules for disciplining body, speech and mind. She resolved to share the fruits of her spiritual virtue in the hope that the boar might be reborn as it wished. Satisfied with Mae Chee Kaew's assurances, and buoyed by her blessings, the boar respectfully took leave and went its way.

Next morning, after sunrise, Mae Chee Kaew met the monks and nuns at the main *sala* and quietly related this bizarre incident. She described the wild boar's story in detail so that they would fully understand the situation and accept the meat out of compassion for the slain animal if the hunter's family were to bring the boar meat later that morning. She urged everyone to eat the meat as a way to honor the animal's generous intentions and, hopefully, to help its consciousness find rebirth as a human being.

Later that morning, the wife of Mr. Dum, the hunter, arrived with some roasted boar meat, which she respectfully offered to Ajaan Khamphan and the monks. When they questioned her about the origin of the meat, her answer confirmed everything that Mae Chee Kaew heard from the wild boar, down to the smallest details. The monks and nuns all partook of the offered meat, hoping that in some way their act of compassion would ease the burden of suffering carried by that unfortunate creature.

Mae Chee Kaew learned about death and rebirth and the craving that connects the two, linking lives in an endless continuum of pain and suffering. She encountered personalities shaped by greed, motivated by anger, and weighed down by the burden of their own *kamma* as they swam helplessly, aimlessly, in a vast sea of delusion. Beings trapped in lower realms of conscious existence have no personal merit, no spiritual virtues on which they can fall back in times of dire need. In previous lives, when those ghosts were born human beings, they failed to develop the habit of selfless giving, and overlooked the protective power of moral restraint. Because as humans they neglected to accumulate a store of virtue for the future, upon death their consciousness plunged into a realm of darkness where it was nearly impossible to generate virtue. Having no recourse to merit of their own making, ghosts and other errant spirits depend on others for salvation. Should virtuous people of the human realm fail to assist them by consciously sharing the merit they make through acts of body, speech and mind, ghosts are left completely destitute, with no means to move on to a favorable rebirth. They must wait, enduring the miserable conditions their actions have produced, until the karmic repercussions of their evil deeds, or of their negligent disdain, have been exhausted. To Mae Chee Kaew, ghosts resembled stray animals, roaming aimlessly through a barren, unearthly landscape, and hounded by their own spiritual poverty with no owner to look after them. For beings stuck with the consequences of evil deeds, it matters little which state of existence they are born into, since their pain and misery continue unabated.

All realms of consciousness, and all living beings originate from the mind. Because of that, it's far better that you focus exclusively on your own mind. There you will find the whole universe.

Ghosts of the Mountain

Under Ajaan Khamphan's leadership, the monastery at Phu Gao Mountain developed into a vibrant spiritual environment where monks and nuns focused diligently on their meditation practice. Ajaan Khamphan had lived under Ajaan Sao's tutelage for several years, and he directed monastic affairs in the same spirit that his famous mentor had. At Phu Gao Mountain, a harmonious sense of fraternity prevailed, everyone living together in unity. The sight of the monks peacefully walking to the village for alms each morning was impressive. The nuns would remain at the monastery, gathered in the open-air kitchen to cook rice and prepare simple dishes to augment the food from the monks' daily alms gathering. The villagers had constructed a long bench at the monastery's entrance. Here the nuns stood and placed the food they had prepared into the monks' bowls on their return from the village. Back in the monastery, at the main *sala*, the monks ate together in silence, seated according to seniority. Having received a blessing, the nuns retired to their quarters to have their meal — also in silence and according to seniority. When the monks finished eating, each monk washed his bowl, dried it thoroughly, replaced its cloth covering, and put it neatly away. The women washed the dishes and the cooking utensils, put everything neatly away and swept the kitchen area clean.

Once the morning duties were complete, all the monastics returned to the secluded environment of their small huts, where they concentrated on meditation, either walking or sitting. The monks and nuns remained in the forest until four p.m. when the afternoon chores began. Upon returning from the forest, they first swept the monastery grounds. When sweeping was finished, they worked together to carry water from the nearby pools to fill the various water vessels: water for drinking, water for washing feet, and water for washing alms bowls and cooking pots. After a quick bath, they resumed their meditation. On nights when no meeting was scheduled, they continued to practice late into the night before retiring.

Normally, Ajaan Khamphan called a general meeting of the monks and nuns once a week, on lunar observance days. Convening at dusk, the whole assembly chanted in unison, intoning sacred verses in praise of the Buddha, Dhamma and Sangha. After the soft resonance of their voices receded, Ajaan Khamphan delivered an inspiring discourse on meditation practice. When he finished speaking, he addressed any questions or doubts expressed by his disciples, and advised them about how they could move their meditation forward. If pressing questions arose on other days, they could seek his personal advice at any convenient time.

Ajaan Khamphan maintained an exemplary mode of practice that inspired reverence in his disciples. He was gentle and gracious, possessing an unassuming manner that was always simple and down-to-earth. His spiritual practice and virtuous conduct reflected a truly calm and peaceful frame of mind. He was highly skilled at attaining states of deep meditative calm, and very knowledgeable about the diversity of phenomena that could be experienced in samādhi. Because of this, his meditative skills were compatible with Mae Chee Kaew's own innate abilities. His mind converged into states of deep samādhi with consummate ease, resulting in extensive contact with beings of the spirit realm. Mae Chee Kaew was able to take advantage of his expertise to further her own skills in the many unusual aspects of samādhi, and was grateful for Ajaan Khamphan's guidance.

The years Mae Chee Kaew spent living at Phu Gao Mountain were a fruitful time for her meditation practice. With each new foray into the invisible world of sentient spirits, she gained increased expertise in the realms of nonphysical existence. With Ajaan Khamphan's assistance, she strengthened her ability to explore varieties of phenomena within the many lowly but subtle nonhuman states of existence that lay beyond the range of normal human perception. These experiences were so many, and varied, that she never tired of exploring the spiritual universe. To her surprise, she discovered that some types of ghosts live in organized communities just as humans do. Contrasting sharply with the vagrant variety, these communities are governed by a leader, who supervises social activities and endeavors to keep peace. Due to the untimely fruition of previous bad *kamma*, some beings, having accumulated a wealth of virtue, are nonetheless reborn into the realm of ghosts. Because their virtuous characters remain, they are able to exercise great moral authority, garnering respect from their peers, who because of their own spiritual poverty, stand in awe of those possessing moral power and authority. In the ghost communities, Mae Chee Kaew found proof that the fruits of goodness were always more powerful than the effects of evil. By the power of virtue alone, one individual is capable of governing a large community.

Mae Chee Kaew also found that the ghost communities were not segregated into groups or castes. Instead, their social hierarchy adhered strictly to the order dictated by the specific consequences of each ghost's *kamma*, making it impossible for them to hold the kind of prejudices that people do. The nature of their ghostly existence, and their social status relative to one another, was always the appropriate retribution for their past misdeeds.

Occasionally, the chief ghost guided Mae Chee Kaew on a tour of his domain, and described the living conditions of different types of ghosts. She was informed that the ghost world has its share of hooligans, too. Bad characters, who cause caused disturbances, were rounded up and imprisoned in an enclosure that humans would call a "jail". He emphasized that the imprisoned ghosts were mean-hearted types, who had unduly disturbed the peace of others, and were sentenced and jailed according to the severity of their offenses. Those who behaved well, lived normal lives as far as their *kamma* allowed. The chief ghost reminded her that the word "ghost" is a designation given by humans. Ghosts were actually just one type of conscious life form among many others in the universe that exists according to its own karmic conditions.

Deva consciousness is another form of sentient existence governed by the laws of *kamma*. Mae Chee Kaew's samādhi meditation introduced her to a rich spectrum of otherworldly experience. Sometimes her consciousness separated from her body and wandered to explore the heavenly realms, or the different levels of the *brahma* world. She visited the various types of subtly formed beings, called *devas*, who exist in a divine hierarchy of increasing subtlety and refinement — beings who have arrived at a fortunate and happy condition as a result of their good *kamma*. She met terrestrial *devas* — luminous deities dwelling in forests, groves and trees — who are born there because of their strong natural affinity to the earthly plane. Although their visible presence existed beyond the range of human senses, they were clearly visible to Mae Chee Kaew's divine eye. She viewed them as beings of contentment whose blissful lives were often preoccupied by sensory pleasures. These enjoyments were the rightful rewards of accumulated virtue. As human beings, they had amassed a store of merit by practicing generous giving, moral restraint and meditation. It propelled them to rebirth in a spiritual heaven, where they lived a blissful existence, enjoying a variety of pleasurable sensory experiences.

Despite the *devas'* virtue, their passive nature gave little chance to actively generate additional good *kamma* to extend their celestial stay. Therefore, once the *devas* exhausted their virtuous capital they could expect to be reborn into the human world, where hopefully their virtuous tendencies would allow them to replenish their supply of merit. In contrast to the ghostly spirits, who are trapped in a cycle of evil and wretched rewards, the *devas* enjoyed an upswing in their karmic fortunes. However, the *devas* do share one thing in common with all sentient beings: the burden of emotional attachments that cause them to be reborn over and over again — without any end in sight.

It's important to understand that these realms exist as dimensions of consciousness and not as physical planes. By characterizing the celestial realms as being progressively "higher" and more refined levels of existence, and the ghostly realms as being correspondingly "lower", the purely spiritual nature of consciousness is erroneously given a material standard. The terms "going up" and "going down" are conventional figures of speech, referring to the movement of physical bodies. These terms have very little in common with the flow of consciousness, whose subtle motion is beyond temporal comparisons. Physically moving up and down requires a deliberate exertion of effort. But when the mind gravitates to higher or lower realms of consciousness, direction is merely a metaphor and involves no effort.

When saying that the heavens and the *brahma* worlds are arranged vertically in a series of realms, this should not be understood in the literal sense — such as, a house with many stories. These realms exist as dimensions of consciousness, and ascent is accomplished spiritually, by attuning the mind's conscious flow to a subtler vibration of consciousness. They are ascended in the figurative sense, by a spiritual means: that is, by the heart which has developed this sort of capability through the practices of generosity, moral virtue and meditation. By saying that hell is "down below", one does not mean going down, physically, into an abyss. Rather, it refers to descent by spiritual means to a spiritual destination. And those who are able to observe the heavens and the realms of hell do so by virtue of their own internal spiritual faculties.

For those skilled in the mysteries of the samādhi, psychic communication is as normal as any other aspect of human experience. Arising from the flow of consciousness, the essential message is transmitted in the language of the heart as fully-formed ideas, which the inquiring individual understands as clearly as if they were words in conventional language. Each thought current emanates directly from the heart, and so conveys the mind's true feelings, and precise meaning, eliminating the need for further clarification. Verbal conversation is also a medium of the heart; but its nature is such that spoken words often fail to reflect the heart's true feelings, so mistakes are easily made in communicating its precise intent. This incongruity is eliminated by using direct heart-to-heart communication.

Keep a close watch over your actions, speech and mind, and conduct yourself with composure. Don't talk too much and create difficulties for yourself. Watch your language, and laugh with restraint.

Nok Kraba Cave

As the years passed, Mae Chee Kaew's meditation developed a definite pattern and direction, and each new encounter with the spirit world reinforced her momentum. She spent countless hours examining the pain and suffering of other living beings, but she neglected to reflect back on herself and the emotional attachments that rooted her in saṁsāra's recurring sequence of death and rebirth. Because her visions involved contact with the mind's internal sense fields, accessed by an inward focus of awareness, she viewed them as explorations of her own mind and its profound psychic capabilities. She believed that by investigating the phenomena arising in her samādhi meditation, she could learn the truth about them, and by that means understand the mental awareness that perceived them. But, although the worlds that appeared in her spiritual visions were realms of being every bit as real and distinctive as the human realm, they were also just as external to the perspective of the meditator, the one who perceived them.

Though not solid and tangible, those phenomena were, by their very nature, objects of perception, and thus extraneous to the awareness that knew them. By focusing exclusively on her visions, Mae Chee Kaew's meditation had become preoccupied with the outer spiritual universe, which caused her to overlook the amazing inner world that existed within her own heart and mind.

Mae Chee Kaew failed to understand this fundamental fault in her practice, and Ajaan Khamphan did not possess enough innate wisdom to point out the mistake. He himself had never progressed beyond the level of samādhi and its psychic effects, so he could not lead her beyond her infatuation with the spiritual dimension. Though his mind was rooted in exceptional powers of concentration, he lacked genuine insight into the fundamentally transient and unsatisfactory nature of spiritual phenomena. Although Mae Chee Kaew believed Ajaan Khamphan to be a competent guide, she had yet to understand her need for a truly exceptional teacher.

Mae Chee Kaew's increasing infatuation with the varieties of conscious existence became strong. She craved for the excitement of new experiences, and greater knowledge — the very craving that causes all sentient beings to wander endlessly in saṁsāra's spiritual universe. Mae Chee Kaew had yet to fully comprehend this lesson about the truth of suffering and its primary cause; and Ajaan Khamphan, with all his powers of concentration, was unable to guide her away from the dangers of strongly favoring samādhi over wisdom. Thus, Mae Chee Kaew became intoxicated by the peaceful tranquility of samādhi, and inadvertently, had become addicted to its wondrous powers of perception.

Mae Chee Kaew lived on Phu Gao Mountain from 1937 to 1945, a period during which the Japanese invaded Thailand and dragged it into an unfolding regional conflict that soon became a major battlefront in World War II. Warplanes flew bombing missions directly over the mountain retreat, and often dropped unused bombs on the mountainside, before landing at a nearby airbase. The periodic and deafening explosions sent the monks and nuns scrambling for safe cover under the overhanging cliff. Only Mae Chee Kaew remained unperturbed, calmly continuing her meditation without fear or annoyance. She was determined to develop her resolve by dedicating her body and mind to the search for Dhamma. She knew that she had to be resolute on the path if she expected to transcend suffering in her lifetime.

During one period of constant bombardment, the disruption to the nuns' meditative environment became so severe that Mae Chee Kaew and several other nuns moved from Phu Gao Mountain to Nok Kraba Cave for more seclusion. Hiking on looping mountain trails for the better part of a day, they arrived at an adjacent mountain range, far removed from the military's normal flight path. Nok Kraba was an extensive network of caves carved into the rugged mountainside, which afforded each nun a separate, secluded stone chamber, where she could practice meditation in quiet solitude.

Emerging from deep samādhi, late on the first night, the outward flow of Mae Chee Kaew's consciousness was confronted by a large serpent-like deity, which she immediately recognized as a *nāga*, a spiritual being whose natural environment was hollow caverns of the earth, and the watery domains beneath them. *Nāgas* had always fascinated Mae Chee Kaew by their ability to change their physical appearance at will, often presenting themselves in human guise. With audacious disregard, the nāga quickly wrapped its spectral coils around her body, arched its reptilian face close to hers and, in a teasing tone, threatened to eat all the nuns before sunrise. Mae Chee Kaew understood the power of not being afraid to die. Face to face with its massive head, she calmly cautioned the nāga to consider the moral repercussions of its rashness. She reminded the nāga that nuns were children of the Lord Buddha, the ideal of spiritual perfection, and they should never be violated. When the nāga maintained its defiant posture, she retorted that if it really intended to eat the nuns, it should take her first. The nāga immediately opened wide its snake-like mouth and prepared to strike her. But, due to the mysterious powers of Mae Chee Kaew's virtue, its mouth suddenly began to burn so hot that it yelled out in pain. Chastened and humbled, the nāga sheepishly assumed the formal appearance of a young man and became friendly.

In the guise of a young man, the nāga agreed to share his abode with the nuns. But he remained a mischievous creature, restlessly flitting about and never staying still. The strange young man liked to sit on a rock in the middle of the cave and play a panpipe very loudly, the sounds echoing playfully around the hollow cavern. But every time he approached Mae Chee Kaew, who was seated in meditation, the sounds from his panpipe became mysteriously muffled, as though the notes could not quite emerge from the mouth of his flute. This enigma puzzled and frustrated him. As time went on, it made him increasingly uncomfortable to think that she could exert control over the sounds he made. At the same time, he grew more and more impressed by her unusual powers, and despaired of ever getting the better of her.

One day, Mae Chee Kaew saw the young man approaching with his panpipe and asked him where he was going. The nāga teased her, saying that he had intended to flirt with a woman in the village, but thought it might be better to flirt with her instead. She shot him a scolding glance and retorted that she was a woman of moral virtue who had no desire for men. She urged him to develop basic moral principles within himself, insisting that moral virtue was the basis of those special qualities that every living being should cherish and hold onto. She explained that moral restraint formed a barrier that prevented living beings from abusing each other's material and spiritual wealth; and that it also protected and maintained one's own inner worth. Without morality's protective restraint, mistreatment and negligence would run so rampant in the world that there would hardly be an island of peace and security left. Mae Chee Kaew urged the young nāga to cease his callous disregard for spiritual values and to reform his moral outlook in line with Buddhist principles. Eliminating such a blight from his heart would produce only peace and happiness for himself and others.

Impressed by her arguments, the young nāga accepted his faults and asked for her forgiveness. Responding to the softening in his heart, Mae Chee Kaew exhorted him to observe the five basic moral precepts:

> First, you must abstain from harming living creatures. By doing so, you will learn to restrain your anger and promote loving kindness. You must abstain from taking things without their owner's consent. By discarding the mentality of a thief, greed is held in check, and renunciation is given room to grow. All improper sexual relations must be abandoned, because refrain-

ing from sexual misconduct helps to subdue sensual lust and develop a spirit of contentment. By abstaining from lying, and always telling the truth, you rein in tendencies towards false speech and emphasize truthfulness in all your dealings. Abstaining from intoxicants avoids harmful mental excitement, and cultivates the development of mindful awareness, which is the basic prerequisite for maintaining all the moral precepts in a smooth and even manner.

Having convinced him to adopt these fundamental moral principles, Mae Chee Kaew taught him that, in addition to moral restraint, generosity and meditation are vitally important elements; that they lay the foundation for spiritual self-reliance in this life, and in all future lives. All living beings are the product of their actions, and they must take full responsibility for the consequences they encounter, for no one else can shoulder that responsibility.

The nuns at Nok Kraba Cave relied on some of the local people to provide them with raw rice and other cooking supplies. They foraged daily for forest greens, edible tubers and wild mushrooms to supplement their diet; but their supply of rice and pickled fish depended on local supporters. The women who supplied them with basic requisites became faithful devotees, and Mae Chee Kaew often rewarded their devotion by relating her meditation experiences as lessons in the value of moral virtue. But when news of her power to tame the nāga reached the wider village community, many local people became fearful and uneasy. Long steeped in animistic beliefs, they were superstitious and wary of anyone whose spiritual powers transcended those of the local deities. They associated Mae Chee

Kaew's taming of the nāga with magical powers, which both awed and frightened them.

Nok Kraba Cave was situated in a wooded region where village people normally hunted and gathered wild plants. Stories of Mae Chee Kaew's powers made the locals feel uneasy about setting foot in that area. Complaints began to emerge. At that time, there were unseasonably heavy rainfalls, day and night, which caused extensive flooding in low-lying villages. The nuns at the cave were soon accused of causing these torrential downpours, and the ensuing floodwaters. It was also suggested that the nuns' presence accounted for recent Japanese army incursions into the region.

A series of unwarranted accusations eventually convinced Mae Chee Kaew that she should leave the area. Although Nok Kraba Cave provided conditions of ideal seclusion, circumstances in the surrounding countryside were less than favorable. She was concerned that misconceptions about her continued presence might cause others further inconvenience. She thus decided to return to the Phu Gao Mountain with her group of nuns.

If you neglect to cultivate your inherent mindfulness and wisdom, striving only half-heartedly, the
obstacles in your path will multiply until they block
all sight of the way, leaving the end of the road
forever in darkness.

Failings of the Spirit

Ajaan Khamphan was the inspiration behind the Phu Gao monastic
community. It was his responsibility to guide the nuns in their daily
practice. This meant frequent contact with the woman renunciants,
meeting them as a group, listening to their experiences and grievances,
and giving them personal advice on a variety of matters. His age and
senior status seemed to preclude the development of worldly attachments between him and the women he taught. But alas, the weaknesses
of the flesh, and failings of the spirit!

A small group of nuns was left behind when Mae Chee Kaew and
the others moved to Nok Kraba Cave. During their absence, Ajaan
Khamphan — with careless disregard for his status as a spiritual mentor — became emotionally involved with one of the remaining nuns.
Although his samādhi meditation allowed him to observe and examine the circumstances of other living beings, Ajaan Khamphan had
neglected to contemplate and penetrate the true nature of his own

being by failing to properly cultivate the faculties of insight and wisdom. He neglected to follow a fundamental tenet of the Buddha's teaching: he did not thoroughly investigate the aggregates of body and mind to see that they are wholly transient, unsatisfactory and devoid of personal essence.

In the deep meditative absorption of samādhi, body and mind merge into a single conscious unity: the mind's essential knowing nature, pure and simple, still and silent. This convergence gives rise to a feeling of pure and harmonious being so wondrous as to be indescribable, and so perfectly pleasurable that it may become addictive. But, regardless of how sublime their experience is, these states of meditative absorption are still defiled by the presence of craving, anger and delusion. Samādhi experiences of this kind will be no more than mundane in nature, and the spiritual insights gained from them will result in mundane wisdom still tainted by those defiling influences.

A mind simplified and unified by samādhi becomes very deep, clear and powerful. Only by directing this focus to the practice of contemplation can true transcendent wisdom be attained. A profoundly insightful investigation of the body, feelings and the mind can uproot afflictions of craving, hatred and delusion, thus realizing the ephemeral and empty nature of all phenomena, eliminating craving and achieving freedom from the cycle of repeated birth and death. Concentration and wisdom must work together, propelling meditation towards its goal like the two wheels of a cart. The calm and concentration of samādhi enables wisdom to reach and remove deep-seated defilements through the use of specialized contemplative techniques. By uprooting these perversions, wisdom, in turn, deepens meditative calm. Thus concentration and wisdom work in tandem to guide the meditator along the Buddha's path to enlightenment.

Emerging from the sublime calm and concentration of samādhi, Ajaan Khamphan withdrew no further than the access gate to the vast external world of spiritual energies. Instead of using samādhi's sharp and clear internal focus to investigate the truth about his own being, and his attachment to the physical and mental components that comprised it, he turned his attention outward to the world of subtle conscious energy fields. Because he did not use liberating wisdom to develop defenses against his baser instincts, he remained subject to sexual craving, and thus gripped by the sensual bonds of deluded existence.

By the time Mae Chee Kaew returned from Nok Kraba Cave, Ajaan Khamphan's infatuation with one of the junior nuns was becoming apparent. But, because of his senior leadership position in the community, and his excellent reputation, the monks and nuns did not dare to reproach him for his indiscretions. Quietly, in private consultations, it was hoped that the affair would soon wane and come to an end. So Ajaan Khamphan's sudden announcement, that he and the junior nun were giving up the robes and returning to lay life as a married couple, caused shock and dismay. Mae Chee Kaew was saddened by his unexpected departure, and disappointed by his failure to live up to the trust that she and the other nuns had placed in his guidance. By that time, the nuns had lived and practiced under his tutelage for nearly eight years. His disrobing not only created an unpleasant scandal in the monastery, but also left a vacuum of monastic leadership, which forced the nuns to consider relocating as soon as possible to a more suitable environment. Suddenly the nuns' spiritual leadership became their own responsibility. Mae Chee Dang and Mae Chee Ying convened a nuns-only meeting, which quickly reached a consensus that they should return to their home village immediately, and seek a convenient location to establish a monastic community strictly for women.

With that goal in mind, Mae Chee Kaew and six other nuns moved to Baan Huay Sai in the spring of 1945. Aware of the nuns' sudden hardship, and sympathetic to their plight, two prominent village elders became their patrons, and presented them with twenty acres of farmland located about a mile south from the village center. Situated higher than the surrounding rice fields, the soil had been used for generations to plant cash crops, such as cotton, hemp and indigo. However, a large portion of the land was covered with tangled stands of bamboo and towering hardwood trees, which afforded the nuns adequate seclusion to pursue their spiritual lifestyle, undisturbed. The nuns graciously accepted the men's generosity and immediately set to work constructing a forest nunnery.

With the help of men and women from Baan Huay Sai, thick patches of undergrowth were cleared to build temporary bamboo shelters. Bamboo sleeping platforms were constructed by splitting sections of bamboo lengthwise, spreading them out flat, then securing them to a bamboo frame with legs, creating a raised sleeping surface of about six feet long, three or four feet wide, and about one and a half feet above the ground. The roofs were thatched with bundles of tall grass that grew abundantly in the surrounding area. One thatched hut was constructed for each nun, and each hut was spaced as far apart from the others as the living area inside the nunnery would allow. Local villagers helped the nuns create paths for walking meditation beside each of their simple huts.

A small but sturdy *sala* was built in a wide, open area that had previously been cultivated. Wooden posts and planks were sawed and trimmed, then nailed into place with wooden pegs to form the basic structure. The roof was a plain grass thatch. A kitchen shelter for preparing meals was constructed nearby, using split bamboo and thatch. An earthenware, wood-fired stove was used for cooking. Basic living requisites were scarce. The nuns used bamboo to make cups and other basic kitchen utensils. As there were no wells on the property, water from a nearby stream was fetched daily and carried to the nunnery compound. Basic commodities, such as shoes, were not available to the nuns, so they used dried betel nut husks to make primitive sandals. Machetes, hoes and shovels were also hard to come by, forcing the nuns to borrow most of their tools from the village. But although Mae Chee Kaew and the nuns lived in conditions of virtual poverty, they lived for the sake of Dhamma and were willing to accept the inconveniences associated with its practice.

The Baan Huay Sai nunnery was small and remote from village life. The training rules were strict and simple. Its living conditions allowed little that was fancy or superfluous. The nuns spent their days in meditation. Every evening, they convened in the main *sala*. Seated respectfully on the hard wooden floor, in a building without comfort or decoration, they chanted sacred verses praising the virtues of the Buddha, Dhamma and Sangha.

Mae Chee Kaew often said that it was much easier to put up with the physical hardships of life as a nun than to be without a good teacher to guide her through the spiritual uncertainties experienced in meditation. The bitter disappointment of seeing Ajaan Khamphan succumb to the power of sensual lust hung like a heavy weight over Mae Chee Kaew's heart. She was seized by a nagging need to understand why meditation had failed to protect him from ordinary, base desires. She found herself grappling with thoughts full of doubt and disquiet. Was her own meditation going in the right direction? Had she overlooked an essential element? Pondering these questions, but lacking answers, she decided that she must search for a truly qualified teacher.

As the two senior-most nuns, Mae Chee Dang and Mae Chee Ying were responsible for the day-to-day running of the nunnery. With their sympathy, and their blessings, Mae Chee Kaew parted company with the group of women she had lived with for eight years, and left the newly-established nunnery to fulfill her mission. Following the rains retreat, and traveling with a junior nun as a companion, Mae Chee Kaew climbed into the Phu Phan foothills north of Baan Huay Sai and continued to hike north along foot trails over tall mountains and through wide valleys, until she reached Ajaan Kongma Chirapuñño's forest monastery high in the eastern-most Phu Phan range.

The human body is a major object of craving and attachment. Suffering is the inevitable consequence. Look at the body! It's a heap of flesh and blood two feet wide and six feet long that is changing every moment.

Body Contemplation

Upon arrival, Mae Chee Kaew met Ajaan Kongma at the monastery's main *sala*. After paying her respects, she told him about her doubts and disquiet regarding the events that clouded her spiritual environment and threatened to undermine her calm and concentration. Her meditation had not gone smoothly since Ajaan Khamphan's disrobing, and she did not understand why. Ajaan Kongma knew, intuitively, that her strong mental focus needed to be directed away from the pursuit of external phenomena, with its attachment to form, and toward a full examination of her own personal being. Because her former teacher had fallen victim to carnal desires, he insisted that she start by initiating a comprehensive review of her physical body. Ajaan Kongma suggested that Mae Chee Kaew begin body contemplation by focusing on the disgusting features and inherent impurities associated with the human body, starting with head hair, body hair, nails, teeth and skin, then working inward to flesh, sinews, bones, marrow, kidneys, heart, membranes, spleen, lungs, intestines, bowels, stomach, feces, bile, phlegm, pus, blood, sweat, fat, tears, skin grease, saliva, mucus, rheum and urine. He insisted that she cease focusing on the external phenomena that had so fascinated her up to then, and turn the full force of her attention inward to investigate the physical components of the bodily presence that she identified as herself.

Respectfully, but hesitantly, Mae Chee Kaew accepted his advice without objection. But she was not satisfied. For her, focusing inward meant repeating the mantra *buddho* until her mind dropped into a state of deep calm. Ajaan Mun taught her this simple practice many years before, and she felt stubbornly reluctant to change. Certain she already knew the way of meditation, she was not prepared to put Ajaan Kongma's advice to a serious test. She stuck doggedly to her usual practice, even though the results continued to bring disappointment and uncertainty. The longer she resisted Ajaan Kongma, the more her mind refused to drop into a fully calm and concentrated state. For months, stubbornness prevented her mind from converging into stillness.

Mae Chee Kaew became exasperated at her lack of progress and felt herself at wit's end. One night, as she walked in meditation, she began to rebuke herself harshly. It had been raining since nightfall, but she refused to go inside. The time had come to teach herself a lesson. Pacing back and forth all night, in the pouring rain, she chastised her stubborn, conceited attitude. Determined to not give up until she had redeemed herself, she examined her faults over and over again to find out why her heart was so unyielding. Although Ajaan Kongma provided her with all the right conditions she needed to progress in meditation, she had doggedly refused to give way.

She knew her stance was unreasonable, and that it must be changed. She asked herself: how can I really know the truth when the mind that I use to acknowledge the truth is so deluded?

The following day, having fully accepted her faults, she resolved to make amends for her intransigence. Solemnly prostrating before the Buddha, she silently asked heartfelt forgiveness of Ajaan Kongma. After preparing her mind by intoning auspicious chants, she began meditating in earnest on the nature of the human body. Mae Chee Kaew contemplated the body by meditating on its inherently impure and repulsive nature. She first reflected on the obvious disgusting features that afflict the body while alive. The nose was constantly filled with mucus, the ears with wax, and the skin exuded sweat and grease; the body continually excreted feces and urine; and, without constant cleaning, it reeked of foul odors and suffered discomfort.

With constant practice, she began to understand clearly that much of her discontent stemmed from embracing the body as the core of her existence and regarding it as a central feature of self and personality. Though it was not obvious in her ordinary consciousness and attitudes, this belief was fundamental and deep-seated, operating at a subliminal and instinctive level of consciousness. Then, by embodying this basic instinct in her conscious activities, she projected a very concrete sense of self into all her actions. She realized that a person's life is often deliberately planned around desires related to the body: constant concern with matters of appearance, fashion, self-esteem and personal comfort. By meditating on the body's impure nature, Mae Chee Kaew began to experience it as inherently repulsive and unstable, something that repelled rather than attracted desire. Through the daily practice of body contemplation, she gradually reduced the craving that had built up around the body, working to free herself from the strong sense of self associated with it.

In her daily meditations, she took the body apart, piece by piece, layer by layer. Investigating skin, she saw it as a thin veneer of tissue covering the body's flesh and internal organs. Although at a casual glance it might appear clean and attractive, closer inspection revealed a scaly, wrinkled layer exuding sweat and grease in abundance. Only constant scrubbing and cleansing made it seem bearable to oneself and to others. Hair may be brushed and styled with care, and admired for its overall appearance; but let a few strands fall into a plate of food and they quickly induce a reflexive loss of appetite. Head hair and body hair are inherently filthy, which is the reason they must be constantly washed and bathed. In fact, nothing that comes into contact with any part of the human body remains clean for long, as the whole body is filthy by its very nature. Due to the filth and odors, accumulated from our bodies, clothing and bedding must be constantly laundered. Even food becomes filthy, once it is ground between the teeth and mixed with the body's secretions. The whole body shares the same repugnant characteristics.

After deeply contemplating the natural filthiness of the body's external features, Mae Chee Kaew investigated its internal organs and their secretions, and its many foul excretions. Having carefully examined hair, nails, teeth and skin, with a growing sense of dismay, Mae Chee Kaew mentally peeled back the outer layer and visualized the body stripped of skin, the underlying flesh exposed, raw and bloody. Close examination of this glistening mass of blood-stained tissue produced nauseating revulsion. Keeping in mind that this sight was no aberration, but rather the reality of the body she had lived with her entire life, she delved deeper into the sinews, the bones and the internal organs. Bands of flesh hugged the bones like raw meat. She envisioned the heart, liver, kidneys, spleen, lungs, stomach, intestines and bowels, all sloshing around in mucus-coated cavities formed within the contour of the ribcage and hip bones, and held in place by a plaster of fibrous membranes. Methodically, she visualized each organ within its own context, each encased in fat and oozing blood and viscous secretions, each enclosing putrid excretions waiting to be discharged.

By using her strong mental focus to explore deeply into the body's internal composition, Mae Chee Kaew saw for the first time, with penetrative insight, the body's true nature. Seeing it clearly with wisdom, she was able to extend that insight to include all bodily substances and realize that they all had the exact same nature. She understood that the entire body was disgusting and repulsive, and that no stable or satisfactory personal essence could be found there. At that moment of profound realization, her mind suddenly dropped into total stillness. A small, faint spot of light, located deep inside her heart, began to flicker and glow. It pulsed and grew brighter, expanding its radiance until her entire conscious being was captured in light and became bright, clear, buoyant and supple.

She withdrew from meditation at dawn and completed her morning chores. A subtle sense of harmony and integration pervaded her every movement. The reserve and hesitancy, that formerly showed in her demeanor, disappeared. She was happy and cheerful as she offered food to the monks for their morning meal. Noticing her dramatic change, Ajaan Kongma announced for all to hear: "Mae Chee Kaew, you're on the right path now. Stay resolute!"

With her meditation back on track, Mae Chee Kaew stayed with Ajaan Kongma for several more months, taking advantage of the opportunity of living with a good teacher to deepen her concentration and cultivate her powers of wisdom. She understood now why Ajaan Khamphan's meditation had failed to protect him from ordinary and base desires rooted in attachment to physical form. She understood the powerful attraction of sensual craving, and she knew the way to neutralize it.

When she finally felt confident that she had developed a solid foundation in her practice, she decided to return to help the other nuns at the Baan Huay Sai nunnery. She was concerned that they still lacked a reliable teacher to guide them on the correct path. She believed that she could now contribute her part and help fulfill that role.

As nuns we must all patiently endure the inevitable hardships of our simple existence without
becoming lazy or disgruntled. Let love and
compassion be your ready response to every
situation.

Ideal Buddhist Nun

Mae Chee Kaew returned to join a healthy spiritual environment
at the Baan Huay Sai nunnery. During her absence, the local Buddhist
laity had come to view the monastic community there as a vital part
of village society. The villagers understood the Buddha's teaching on
generosity and virtue as an invitation to the wider community to
support the religious life of ordained renunciants. The presence of
practicing nuns within rural Phu Tai society was a stronghold of
goodness, a genuine "field of merit" that all people could cultivate
for their own benefit.

The Baan Huay Sai nunnery beckoned women seeking spiritual
liberation and nurtured the spiritual lifestyle of the ideal Buddhist
nun. She was a woman who stepped out from ordinary society,
renouncing a household life of husband, children and family to take
a vow of complete sexual abstinence. Her appearance reflected her
changed status: her head was shaved, and she wore white monastic

robes. Adopting a wholly religious path, she abandoned the normal means of livelihood, and instead depended on the generosity of others to supplement the few possessions she owned.

The basic spirit of a nun's practice was found in the solemn rectitude of the moral precepts, the training rules that guide the life of the Buddhist renunciant, and her path to spiritual liberation. Because the precepts are the bedrock on which all spiritual progress rests, ordained followers of the Buddha's teaching have always attached great importance to their observance. The moral training's true worth lies in its power to cut through the karmic causes and conditions that bind living beings to the cycle of birth and death. The precepts provide a foundation for Buddhist practice that closes the door to actions carrying painful karmic consequences. At the same time, it upholds the purity of mind and deeds that lead to freedom from suffering. The moral precepts also ensure high standards of purity within the monastic community, enabling it to flourish internally and to function as an inspiring model for lay society.

In the Baan Huay Sai nunnery, a nun's conduct adhered strictly to eight basic precepts. In practice, she never harmed living creatures; she never took what had not been given; she led an entirely celibate life; she never used false, divisive, harsh or frivolous speech; she never took intoxicants; she never ate food after midday; she never amused herself with entertainment, or adorned herself with jewelry and cosmetics; and she never rested on high or luxurious beds. In essence, these simple rules articulate a way of life characterized by restraint and renunciation, leading to detachment and insight.

The first four training rules — strictures against killing, stealing, lying and sexual activity — delineate the moral foundation in which

Buddhist monastic life is rooted. The other precepts are principles of spiritual training that help to create the conditions for a calm body and a clear mind. As such, they are merely an expansion of the basic four. When a nun is pure in observing the spirit of the first four, the other precepts are easy to keep. On the other hand, their infraction is considered a major offence. Seeking to solve the problem of suffering in any way that harms other living creatures is a misguided manifestation of anger and delusion. Taking what is not freely given betrays the fundamental relationship of trust existing between nuns, who undertake lives of ascetic practice, and those who, in good faith, offer them material support. Failure to maintain vows of celibacy undermines a defining characteristic of Buddhist nuns: their renunciation of ordinary family life. Beyond that, sexual abstinence helps to channel their energies toward higher spiritual attainments. False or frivolous speech undermines truthfulness and destroys trust within the spiritual community, among the lay supporters and most of all within one's own mind.

The nature of true moral virtue is subtle and complex — so complex that it cannot be attained merely by reference to precepts and rules of conduct. Ultimately, moral virtue is not measured in terms of adherence to external rules, but as an expression of the mind's pure intentions. The basic goal of the Buddhist path is to eliminate from the mind all impure intentions. Thus, true virtue can only be achieved by following a path of training that succeeds in rooting out greed, anger and delusion. Moral precepts are a necessary part of the training; but the practice of moral virtue cannot fully accomplish its goal unless it is oriented toward the practice of meditation. Properly nourished with virtuous intentions, the mind quickly and easily develops meditative calm and clarity. Therefore, a nun who abides by the precepts experiences an unblemished and spacious happiness within.

Life at the Baan Huay Sai nunnery was quiet and simple, emphasizing the development of mindfulness in each daily activity. Through her meditation skills, Mae Chee Kaew began to assume an expanded leadership role in advising junior nuns on the mode and direction of their mental training. She strove to lead by example, setting the tone for the others by rising at three in the morning and walking in meditation until five. With the sun's first early morning rays illuminating the pathway to the outdoor kitchen, she joined the other nuns to prepare the day's food. The fragrant aroma of food and incense mingled softly in the morning air. A generous portion of their cooking was set aside to be offered as alms to monks from a nearby monastery. After respectfully placing the food into the monks' bowls, the nuns quietly gathered at the main *sala*, and ate their morning meal together in complete silence. They reflected on the nature of the food set before them. Viewing it as no more than a necessary requisite supporting their religious lifestyle, they developed an attitude of contentment with whatever they received. Following the meal, the nuns washed their utensils and cleaned up the kitchen area before retiring to their separate huts to continue their meditation practice. Because they ate only once, they were free to focus exclusively on their inner development for the remainder of the day.

Having completed the morning's chores, Mae Chee Kaew turned her undivided attention to meditation. Retiring to a small cabin in a secluded section of the nunnery, where gigantic clumps of bamboo mingled with teak and mahogany trees, she entered a calm, quiet environment free of external distractions. Under the leafy canopy, on a shady space of level ground, the local villagers had made a walking meditation track by clearing a broad swath of earth and smoothing it out flat. After sweeping the path clean, Mae Chee Kaew stood erect and alert at one end and joined her hands just below the waist, the palm of the right hand gently overlapping and clasping the back of the left. With eyes downcast, and mind focused, she paced back and forth, from one end of the path to the other, pivoting and turning in one fluid and easy motion at the end of each span. She found the continuous movement of walking helpful in relieving the drowsiness and mental torpor induced by a full stomach. Harmonizing the repetition of *buddho* with each footfall, she completed several hours of continuous walking every morning. As her mind became absorbed in *buddho*, and her concentration deepened, the rhythm and pace of movement began to change, adapting fluidly to the steady current of awareness that had developed. Moving in perfect unison, as a single entity, her whole body appeared to glide effortlessly along the path, as though on a soft cushion of air.

Refreshed and invigorated, Mae Chee Kaew then sat under the shade of a spreading *phayom* tree at the side of the path to continue her meditation until three p.m., when the nuns took up their afternoon chores. Together they swept the grounds of the nunnery, filled the water jars with water from the newly-dug well, and then went off into the nearby woods to collect mushrooms, bamboo shoots and other edible plants for the kitchen. After an early evening bath, Mae Chee Kaew joined the other nuns at the main *sala* for the evening chanting. When the chanting was finished, each nun returned to her small hut to continue walking and sitting meditation in peace and solitude of the surrounding forest. Mae Chee Kaew walked in meditation again for several hours before retiring to her hut to sit until late at night.

In the first few months after her return from Ajaan Kongma, Mae Chee Kaew continued her diligent focus on body contemplation. But gradually her attention drifted away from the body as a meditation subject, and toward her previous habits of external focus. Body contemplation went against the grain of her inherent spiritual tendencies; and in the end she succumbed to the natural momentum of her dynamic and venturesome mind. As soon as she closed her eyes, she felt herself falling down a precipice. A window to the universe opened up, and suddenly, she was off on another adventure.

Each person who is born must die and be reborn again and again in a cycle of suffering and hardship. Perhaps we'll die in the morning, perhaps in the evening, we don't know. But we can be certain that death will come when the time is ripe.

Pilgrimage

Faithfully each year, when the cold season ended and the sun began rising higher in the southern sky and warmer days lengthened, Mae Chee Kaew led a small band of nuns on a pilgrimage to visit Ajaan Mun, who was living in the neighboring province of Sakon Nakhon. The first late-winter rains had fallen by then, leaving the mango trees bursting with a constellation of blossoms and humming with swarms of nectar-hungry bees. Preparations had to be made for the journey, a 12-day trek over the Phu Phan Mountains, down into Sakon Nakhon province, proceeding along broken, hilly terrain, and into the broad valley of Baan Pheu Na Nai. The supplies were heavy and cumbersome, so the nuns carried only enough food to get them over the high mountains, where settlements were scarce. When their meager supplies ran out, they would rely on the generosity of small, far-flung farming communities that were often located a full day's hike from one another. Uncooked rice was packed in plaited bamboo baskets. The pungent pickled fish, used as flavoring, was stored in clay jars sealed with fresh bee's wax. Dried meat and fish completed their diet, along with the wild forest plants they foraged on the way.

The nuns left Baan Huay Sai Nunnery walking in a single file with Mae Chee Kaew in the lead. In addition to food, each nun carried a few basic necessities in her shoulder bag and an umbrella-tent to protect her from the elements at night. Simple home-made sandals sheltered her feet from rough ground and sharp stones. A plain cotton cloth covered her shaved head, protecting it from direct sunlight.

By the end of the first day, the nuns had reached the Phu Phan foothills. The jungle was teeming with bears, tigers and snakes, with only a scattering of human settlements located in crude pockets of cultivation. The weather was difficult and unpredictable. Still, the land was beautiful, verdant and rich, thick with bamboo and rosewood, and carpeted by grasses, ferns and wild flowers — a landscape of massive trees rooted in tangled undergrowth. Spacious vistas at mountain passes gave way to vaulted canopies of foliage and creepers, and then to myopic tunnels of chaotic vegetation. Protruding on ridges, undulating outcrops of black sandstone flowed over hillsides, breaking and folding into deep crevices where the trail could easily disappear for an inexperienced traveler.

While passing a small village, the weary travelers could hear an offer of food and support. Grateful, and with love in their hearts, the nuns took what little they were offered from the impoverished donors and searched for a secluded stream to bathe and camp for the night. Each nun sought shelter under a hand-crafted umbrella, suspended from a tree limb, with a thin cotton tent-cloth draped gracefully to the ground and encircling a bed of straw and dry leaves on which she could meditate for the night.

Some nights, in the small hours, Mae Chee Kaew dreamed of Ajaan Mun. His stern but caring face peered at her mischievously, as if to say, "Where have you been all this time? What's taking you so long? Can't you see I grow older by the day?" She shuddered, hearing the urgency and the steely resolve in his voice.

Each morning the nuns partook of a single, simple meal of steamed-cooked sticky rice, kneaded into bite-size lumps and dipped in fermented fish paste. Their meals were sometimes augmented with slivers of dried meat and fish, freshly dug roots and tubers, and a selection of forest herbs, spices, fruits and berries. Their daily repast was just enough to sustain body and mind on the long march to nightfall, as the nuns traveled one step at a time, one mindful moment after another, and always in the present.

After almost a fortnight of hiking along timeworn footpaths over mountains and through valleys, past fallow rice fields and orchard groves, Mae Chee Kaew and her companions finally arrived in the vicinity of Ajaan Mun's forest retreat on the afternoon of the twelfth day. They were met first by the residents of Nong Pheu village, gracious women bustling with hospitality who helped the nuns bathe and wash their dusty robes. Once refreshed, the nuns made their final hike along the gently sloped and winding path to Ajaan Mun's monastery.

Ajaan Mun's monastic community was nestled in a dense jungle at the upper end of a broad valley. The valley was surrounded by overlapping mountain ranges that seemed to stretch on forever, making it an ideal location for the kind of solitude which the *dhutanga* monks sought. Clusters of thatched huts dotted the mountain ridges where groups of five or six families eked out a living growing crops and hunting game. Many *dhutanga* monks relied on those remote communities for their daily alms food, just as Mae Chee Kaew and her nuns had done on their journey.

The nuns found Ajaan Mun seated in the central *sala*, chewing betel nut. He seemed to be expecting them. Eagerly, the nuns kicked off their sandals, quickly washed their feet with scoops of potted water and scrambled up the wooden steps to meet him. Always pleased at the sight of Mae Chee Kaew, Ajaan Mun roared out a rough greeting in the Phu Tai dialect, threw his head back and laughed. The nuns prostrated in unison before him, making three fluid bows, their white robes swishing gently with each graceful movement. They sat respectfully to one side with their legs tucked neatly beneath them, smiling softly, expectantly, and mindful of his fearsome reputation.

Ajaan Mun never failed to greet Mae Chee Kaew and her students with warmth and courtesy. After exchanging pleasantries and giving encouragement, he arranged for them to stay overnight in a secluded bamboo grove on the monastery's edge. Tonight, they would sleep once more sleep in their umbrella-tents on piles of bamboo leaves. Tomorrow, he would have the villagers construct sturdy platforms of split bamboo for his guests. He always welcomed Mae Chee Kaew as if she were part of the family, and insisted she stay as long as she liked.

Each morning, after he finished his meal and the nuns had eaten theirs, Ajaan Mun gathered them around his seat and began to speak in a crisp, clear voice, chiding them for their laziness, or urging zeal and determination. They were lively, animated conversations. He was particularly interested to hear of Mae Chee Kaew's meditation adventures, strange and mystical tales of disparate realms of life and consciousness. Though he rarely contradicted the accuracy of her observations, he tried gently and persuasively to reverse the focus of her mind's eye inward. Mae Chee Kaew was obviously enthusiastic about her remarkable ability and proud to show off her otherworldly exploits. Ajaan Mun was a master of all worlds, seen and unseen, known and unknown to all but the purest of minds; and while he was impressed by her mind's capabilities, he was equally concerned of its risks. Better than anyone, he knew the danger of visions and the illusion of knowledge. The pure mind knows all things, equally, evenly, but attaches itself to nothing. To help Mae Chee Kaew shift her perspective and experience the true wonders of her mind, Ajaan Mun taught her many different methods. However, ingrained tendencies form habits, and habits have their own inevitable momentum. Many years before, Ajaan Mun foresaw that a dynamic teacher would appear in the future to steer Mae Chee Kaew along the right path. And so, in the end, it was left to fate to determine the time and circumstances of her awakening.

Year after year, Mae Chee Kaew saw the tide of *anicca* — the law of ubiquitous change — overtaking Ajaan Mun's physical form. His body was ageing quickly now, though his mind remained a diamond of the finest brilliance. Mae Chee Kaew had always maintained a very close spiritual relationship with him. The fact that her nunnery was mountains and valleys away mattered little, for she was often aware of his presence in her nightly meditation. His appearance was radiant and sublime, giving no indication that he had endured the onslaught of a grave illness shortly after she left him that spring. But as time passed and his condition rapidly declined, the tenor of his nocturnal visits changed. There was a poignant urgency in his voice when he insisted she hurry to visit him one last time before it was too late. It frightened her to think that he was dying, but she was aware of the world's true nature — the nature of life, and of death — and of their inevitable uncertainty. Still, she procrastinated. On many occasions, visions of Ajaan Mun warned her to come without delay. Perhaps it was hope for his recovery that kept her from accepting the serious-ness of his illness, and the nearness of his death. Perhaps she was preoccupied with her own spiritual quest, and aware of his watchful presence. Or perhaps she was simply lazy. Whatever the reason, she procrastinated. She occasionally told the nuns to prepare for another long trek, but she always neglected to set a date. So, despite his ad-monitions and repeated warnings, Mae Chee Kaew was still at Baan Huay Sai the night Ajaan Mun passed away.

The hour was past midnight. Mae Chee Kaew had been seated, meditating as usual since nightfall. In a moment of deep, motionless calm, Ajaan Mun's radiant presence appeared one last time. His coun-tenance flashed, his tone fierce and so direct that it shattered her composure. With a voice like a thunderclap, he admonished her for being negligent. Out of pure compassion, with the love of a father for his daughter, he had exhorted her repeatedly to rush to his bedside. Now it was too late. Soon he would pass into final Nibbāna and depart this world forever. When she went to see him, she would find only a corpse, which had no consciousness remaining to acknowledge her. Negligence, laziness, another lost opportunity.

"Don't let defiling emotions take over, Mae Kaew. They are the source of an endless procession of births and deaths. Never assume that mental defilements are somehow harmless, or trivial. Only a heart of courage and determination can defeat their tricks. Look inside and let Dhamma be your guide.

"Earth, water, fire and wind; ground, sky, mountains and trees; heavens, hells and hungry ghosts — these are not the paths, the fruitions or Nibbāna. They do not reveal the truth to you. Do not expect to find it there. They are all true within their own natural spheres, but they don't contain the truth you should be seeking. Delighting in them will merely lead you endlessly around the vicious cycle. Stop spinning. Look within yourself. The truth of Dhamma arises only within the heart. It shines only within the heart, like the full moon in a cloudless sky."

Long before the first light of dawn, Mae Chee Kaew withdrew from samādhi meditation with a cold sweat clinging to her white robes. She was tired and disheartened. She felt a hole in the bottom of her heart. She felt a deep loss of her teacher, her pride and her hope. She laid down to rest but she could not sleep — the energy of the emotion was too strong. She wept softly to herself, breathing slowly and deeply to ease the pain. When the first rays of light spilled into her room at dawn, she rose, gathered her composure and moved briskly in the morning chill to meet the nuns at the main sala. Tears formed as she opened her mouth to speak. His vision, his admonition, his teaching, his death — the story of Ajaan Mun's final appearance poured from her lips and rolled down her cheeks. The nuns had known Mae Chee Kaew long enough to believe in her extraordinary gifts of prescience. Still, they were reluctant to accept the sad news so readily.

As Mae Chee Kaew finished speaking, and the nuns huddled together with conflicting emotions, the village headman bounded up the *sala* steps and blurted out, "Khun Mae, have you heard the news yet? Have you heard the news?" He took a deep breath and exhaled slowly; and said, almost in a whisper, "Ajaan Mun passed away last night in Sakon Nakhon. I heard it on the radio just a few minutes ago. They said he died late in the night, at 2:23 a.m." As the nuns wept uncontrollably, he apologetically added, "I'm sorry, Khun Mae. I thought you should know."

Ajaan Mun died on November 10, 1949, two days after Mae Chee Kaew's forty-eighth birthday. By the time his funeral ceremony was held in late January, she had already traveled once to Sakon Nakhon to pay her respects. Kneeling before his casket, its entire front panel made of glass, she gazed upon his lifeless remains and felt a twinge of remorse. Quietly, silently, she asked his forgiveness for all her past transgressions: *"Mahā There pamādena…"*, and resolved for the future: no more negligence, no more laziness, no more regrets.

As the cremation day approached, Mae Chee Kaew and the nuns made the long trek to Sakon Nakhon one more time. They arrived just in time to see the monks solemnly carry Ajaan Mun's casket from the temple pavilion to the funeral pyre. Mae Chee Kaew, along with many in the large crowd, wept openly as his body passed by. He had long since entered the sublime, pure land of Nibbāna. Never again would he return to physical, bodily existence — the land of tears and lamentation. She watched, spellbound, as the fire was lit at midnight, and felt his unmistakable presence as a small moon-lit cloud began to rain ever so gently on the burning pyre.

Part Three
Essence

Seeing stubbornness in themselves, intelligent people recognize stubbornness. Seeing gloom, they recognize gloom. Seeing delusion, they recognize that too. They look for their own faults; they don't try to fault other people.

Intersecting Karmic Paths

Mae Chee Kaew redoubled her efforts. She always started her meditation with a resolve to redirect her focus inward and hold it there, to fix it in her heart. But focusing inward for Mae Chee Kaew meant going into a mental freefall. As soon as she closed her eyes, the bottom dropped away and she felt herself falling into space as though she were falling from a cliff, or down into a well. Fragmented images flashed by for a few moments; and then, utter stillness, calm, contentment... But hidden beneath the stillness was an almost reflexive momentum that soon rebounded her flow of consciousness back into the realm of fragmented imagery. Suspended in this fluid mental space, Mae Chee Kaew felt right at home. She had learned to navigate its mysterious passageways with ease. Following a flash of recognition, a presence, an emotion, a disembodied consciousness, she plunged into another world, the myriad realms of sentient existence. Her desire to understand the truth drove her to observe newer heights, and depths, of saṁsāric being. Constantly observant, she noticed celestial forms, their means of dialogue, and their habits, customs and beliefs. Sharply focusing her divine eye, she probed the spiritual universe for insight or clues that might help her discover the truth of the Buddha's teaching. Again, she was falling victim to the outward tendency of her conscious mind.

As she struggled on her own to deepen her meditation, Mae Chee Kaew was unaware that one of Ajaan Mun's close disciples had just then reached the final stage of realizing the truth of Dhamma, and that their karmic paths would soon intersect.

Ajaan Mahā Boowa Ñāṇasampanno headed into the Phu Phan Mountains following Ajaan Mun's cremation. Several days of hiking brought him to Wat Doi Dhammachedi, Ajaan Kongma's mountain retreat, where several years earlier Mae Chee Kaew had struggled so spiritedly with her stubborn temperament. A consummate spiritual warrior, Ajaan Mahā Boowa attacked the defilements of his mind as though they were a mortal enemy, accepting nothing short of their utter capitulation. For years his meditation had resembled all out war, each seated session like hand-to-hand combat, each walking session a life-or-death struggle. One by one his inner adversaries were beaten into retreat, no mercy given, no prisoners taken. Still he pursued them relentlessly, searching for the hidden source of their power. Beginning with the most obtrusive and obvious mental defilements — the foot soldiers — he cleared a path and battled his way through until he reached the elite troops, the subtler and more cunning deceptions that encircled and protected their elusive commander, the fundamental delusion about his mind's true essence.

The primal delusion that mobilizes the forces of greed and anger is always cunningly concealed in the deepest recess of the heart. Being the chief ruler of the entire saṁsāric realm, delusion is defended to the death by its formidable army of mental defilements. To liberate the mind from its scourge, these guardians must be disarmed and stripped of their deceptive power. To breach the ramparts of his own fundamental delusion, Ajaan Mahā Boowa rallied his own supreme forces, mindfulness and wisdom, and lay siege to delusion's inner sanctum. Confronting the defenses with mindfulness, and disabling them with wisdom, his forces methodically closed in on the enemy stronghold. When all the mental defilements were finally eliminated, the last one left in the heart was the great commander — the underlying delusion that creates and perpetuates the cycle of birth and death. The final assault had begun. With a lightning strike of extraordinary power and brilliance, the last vestiges of delusion were destroyed, causing the entire edifice of saṁsāric existence to collapse and disintegrate, leaving the mind's true essence absolutely pure, and free of all defilement. Another fully-enlightened arahant had arisen in the world.

In that same year, following the annual rains retreat, Mae Chee Kaew's meditation was witness to a prophetic vision of the moon and its surrounding stars falling from the sky. She interpreted the vision to mean that an exceptional meditation teacher, followed by a group of gifted disciples, would soon arrive at Baan Huay Sai. She became very excited, convinced by the nature of her vision that this monk would be the meditation teacher Ajaan Mun told her about many years before.

Mae Chee Kaew confidently informed the other nuns that the coming year would see the arrival of a group of *dhutanga* monks, led by a great meditation master. She did not yet know who the monk was, but she had perceived an unmistakable sign. She compared his coming to the time Ajaan Mun brought a group of monks to Baan Huay Sai when she was a young girl. In the following months, just as she predicted, several groups of *dhutanga* monks came and went. With hope and anticipation, Mae Chee Kaew walked to their forest encampment to greet them and pay her respects. But each time she left disappointed, certain that they were not the monks represented in her vision.

In January 1951, Ajaan Mahā Boowa wandered down from the Phu Phan mountains, leading a group of *dhutanga* monks. They camped in the thickly wooded foothills to the north of Baan Huay Sai. They camped under trees, in caves, on mountain ridges and under overhanging cliffs, living simply and practicing meditation in the traditional *dhutanga* fashion. Ajaan Mahā Boowa chose to stay in a cave on the gently sloping crest of a mountain ridge, well over a mile from the village center. He took residence in Nok An Cave, with a lone novice as his attendant. Nok An Cave was a long, broad cavern that nestled snugly under a prominent overhanging cliff, and was paved at its entrance with flat, outspreading rocks. The living quarters were cool and well-ventilated, and the environment radiated natural peace and harmony.

When news of Ajaan Mahā Boowa's arrival reached her, Mae Chee Kaew led several nuns up a steep and winding mountain trail to meet him. The high ground at the ridge's peak flattened into outcrops of black sandstone that followed the undulating contours of the ground to the cave's entrance. Approaching the entrance, Mae Chee Kaew spotted Ajaan Mahā Boowa seated on a flat boulder just outside. Barely able to contain her delight, she quickly turned and, with a joyful smile, whispered, "That's him! That's the great meditation master I told you about!"

Cautiously, with gestures of respect, the nuns drew near Ajaan Mahā Boowa. They dropped to their knees in front of his seat and gracefully prostrated three times. After exchanging pleasantries with him, Mae Chee Kaew mentioned that long ago, when she was still a girl, she had met Ajaan Mun. She described in detail the scene from her childhood, recounting how Ajaan Mun taught her meditation, and how he later forbade her to meditate in his absence. Out of deep respect for Ajaan Mun, she had foregone any attempts at meditation for many years. It was only after she had become a nun that she started meditating again in earnest.

As a close disciple of Ajaan Mun, Ajaan Mahā Boowa was puzzled. Why would Ajaan Mun have forbidden her to meditate? As soon as she told Ajaan Mahā Boowa about her prolific visions, he quickly realized the reason. When she met Ajaan Mahā Boowa, Mae Chee Kaew had been deeply engrossed in encountering strange and unusual phenomena during her samādhi meditation for more than ten years. If she failed to see visions, she believed she gained little benefit from meditation. Being wholly addicted to these spiritual adventures, she had convinced herself that they represented the true path to Nibbāna, and to the end of all suffering. At once, Ajaan Mahā Boowa recognized her fundamental mistake. Without a highly-skilled meditation teacher to restrain her excesses, she was easily led by her venturesome and dynamic mind to misinterpret her experiences and misdirect her efforts towards a false goal. But he also knew that someone with a powerful mind like hers could progress very quickly in Dhamma, once she learned to properly train her mind. Ajaan Mahā Boowa realized that, like Ajaan Mun, Mae Chee Kaew would be able to use her unusual abilities in profound and amazing ways to free herself from suffering and to help other living beings do the same.

From that time on, Mae Chee Kaew regularly visited Ajaan Mahā Boowa at his mountain retreat. Once a week, late in the afternoon on lunar observance days, she and the nuns of Baan Huay Sai ascended the winding mountain trail to pay their respects to Ajaan Mahā Boowa, and then to hear him deliver an inspirational discourse on Dhamma. When he finished, he asked the nuns about their meditation. Every time Ajaan Mahā Boowa questioned Mae Chee Kaew, she spoke only of the extraordinary phenomena, the variety of ghosts and disembodied spirits she encountered. Her extensive travels in the heaven and hell realms gave her firsthand knowledge of the various beings that lived there. She described the ghosts' mental states and life circumstances in detail, and how their previous *kamma* resulted in their birth to these realms.

It was apparent that Mae Chee Kaew was captivated by these strange visions and the unusual knowledge they revealed. This worried Ajaan Mahā Boowa. He was astonished by her extraordinary psychic abilities, but realized that she did not yet have sufficient control over her mind to meditate safely on her own. Instead of sending her attention out to perceive external phenomena, he wanted her to learn how to keep it firmly focused within her own body and mind. Only by keeping her awareness firmly centered inside could she overcome the mental defilements that were preventing her from taking her meditation to a higher level.

Ajaan Mahā Boowa explained that the initial aim of meditation is to develop Right Samādhi. To practice samādhi correctly, she had to relinquish her obsession with thoughts and images that entered her awareness. She had to free the mind from the unnecessary limitations caused by being habitually focused on the contents of thought and imagination. Through the right practice of samādhi she could directly experience the mind's essential knowing nature, which would allow her to examine physical and mental phenomena with detached objectivity. The mind's knowing essence is an awareness more vast than the perception of images, thoughts and feelings. It is an unobstructed inner space that contains everything, but retains nothing. Once this power of mental awakening is developed, it can be renewed and deepened without limit. Before that breakthrough occurs, over-attention to external phenomena distracts from the primary purpose: reaching the source of awareness itself.

In the beginning, Ajaan Mahā Boowa simply listened as Mae Chee Kaew related her unusual adventures. He carefully gauged the conditions of her mind's spiritual energy, and then gently tried to persuade her to redirect the flow of her conscious awareness inward to its original source. He repeated that consciousness is a function of mind, not the essence of mind. She must let go of consciousness, and its conditioned awareness, to let the mind's true essence shine forth.

When Ajaan Mahā Boowa noticed after several weeks that she was ignoring his advice, he insisted that she keep her mental focus entirely inside for some of the time during meditation. She could still direct her awareness to observe external phenomena from time to time. But, she must also force it to stay at home at other times. He urged her to learn how to control her mind so that she would be able to direct the flow of consciousness either inward or outward, as she wished.

Because her visions involved contact with the mind's internal sense fields, Mae Chee Kaew viewed them as being explorations of her own mind. She believed that by investigating the phenomena arising in her samādhi meditation, she could learn the truth about the conscious awareness that perceived them. Stubbornly set in her ways, and reluctant to alter her approach, she began openly resisting Ajaan Mahā Boowa's teaching, arguing that her meditation was already providing her with knowledge and insight of a profound nature. She saw no reason to change. Ajaan Mahā Boowa patiently explained that the phenomena she witnessed were merely things that existed naturally in the universe. They were no more special than things seen with open eyes. Although the worlds that appeared in her spiritual visions were realms of being just as real and distinctive as the human realm, they were also just as external to the awareness that perceived them. Though not solid and tangible like material objects of perception, they were still separate from the awareness that knew them. Essentially, from the observer's viewpoint, there was no difference between physical objects and spiritual ones. All were objects in the external world. He wanted her to reverse the direction of her focus, halting the outward flow of consciousness and turning inwards to realize the true essence of mind — the very source of awareness itself.

Mae Chee Kaew continually countered that, unlike the physical eye, the inner eye could see unusually strange and wonderful things. The inner eye was capable of seeing many varieties of ghosts and other disembodied beings. It could see and interact with *devas* in all the heavenly realms. It could see past life connections and accurately foresee future events. She maintained that this sort of knowledge and vision was superior to that perceivable by the ordinary senses.

Ajaan Mahā Boowa did not tolerate stubbornness indefinitely. Abruptly changing tack, he demanded, with a powerful and vigorous insistence, that she prevent her mind from venturing out to perceive spiritual phenomena. Such misdirected awareness would never help her overcome the fundamental causes of birth, ageing, sickness and death. He reminded her that he was teaching her this for her own good, and he made it clear that he expected his instructions to be obeyed.

Ajaan Mahā Boowa's admonition notwithstanding, Mae Chee Kaew felt so confident of her own knowledge and understanding that she continued meditating as before, and later argued with him again about its true value. Exasperated and thoroughly weary of her intransigence, Ajaan Mahā Boowa became fierce. He raised his voice and gestured forcefully as he forbade her to direct her awareness outward to encounter external phenomena. In no uncertain terms, he ordered her to reverse the direction of her focus, and keep it centered inside at all times. He was uncompromising. Only by accepting his teaching and practicing it diligently could she eliminate the defiling elements that deluded her mind.

Late one afternoon, as Mae Chee Kaew stubbornly continued to argue her case, Ajaan Mahā Boowa abruptly broke the conversation off, and curtly dismissed her from his presence. He told her point-blank to leave the cave immediately, and to never return. Uttering harsh and fiery words, he chased her off in front of the other nuns.

Mae Chee Kaew was taken aback by the intensity of his verbal attack and the seriousness of his tone. Such an outcome had never occurred to her. Mae Chee Kaew left Ajaan Mahā Boowa's cave in tears, feeling utterly devastated, her confidence shattered. With his stern reprimand still ringing in her ears, she made the long trek back to the nunnery feeling that she would never see him again.

Despondently, Mae Chee Kaew trudged down the steep mountain path, gripped by her dilemma. She had been convinced from the first moment she saw Ajaan Mahā Boowa that she could depend on him as the right teacher to guide her meditation. Now that he had unceremoniously chased her away, who could she depend on for expert guidance? After so many years of searching for such a teacher, Mae Chee Kaew now felt hopelessly lost.

As knowledge concerning your mind's true essence blossoms and blooms within your heart, the end of the long road of suffering will gradually come into view.

A Portent of Dhamma

Walking through the nunnery's entrance in the looming dusk, Mae Chee Kaew proceeded quickly to her small bamboo hut. She needed time alone, time to digest the day's traumatic events. But the familiar space inside the hut felt oddly different now, as though she were suddenly a stranger in her own house. As night slowly settled in around her pensive mood, the moon and stars appeared dimmer and less welcoming than before. Shaken, and uncomfortably unsure of herself, Mae Chee Kaew sensed an urgent need to make amends.

Reflecting on her predicament, Mae Chee Kaew eventually realized that Ajaan Mahā Boowa had a legitimate reason for driving her away; she had deliberately refused to heed his advice, or make any effort to change. The more deeply she pondered, the more clearly she understood that her own conceited attitude was to blame. He obviously had a good reason for disapproving her style of meditation and pointing her in a different direction. But, why couldn't she accept his teaching? She had really gotten nowhere by willfully resisting his advice in deference to her own selfish indulgence. What if she were to simply do what he told her to do? She should at least try, instead of always stubbornly refusing. Seeing her mistake, she reproached herself: you accepted him as your teacher; so, why can't you accept what he teaches? Just do what he says and you'll know for yourself the truth of his teaching. As dawn approached, the fog of uncertainty began to clear, and she decided she must quickly redeem herself. She would force her mind to succumb to the teaching, and willingly accept the consequences.

The next morning, shortly after the meal, Mae Chee Kaew excused herself from the regular duties and immediately retired to her hut. With a sense of grave urgency, she seated herself in meditation, intending to force her awareness to remain strictly within the confines of her body and mind. She was determined to prevent her mind from focusing outward to become involved with any external phenomena whatsoever. She had perceived ghosts and *devas* and other disembodied spirits for so long that they no longer held special significance for her. Every time she focused her attention outward in meditation, she encountered nonphysical beings. Although she saw nonphysical beings in the same way that other people see with their physical eyes, Mae Chee Kaew had never gained any real benefit from that ability. The defilements constantly polluting her mind remained unaffected. Only by concentrating inward, and closely observing the movement of her conscious mind, could she understand those mental impurities and overcome their influence.

Fully accepting this principle, she focused her attention solely on the internal recitation of *buddho*, and continued until all thoughts ceased and her flow of consciousness converged into single-minded concentration deep within her heart. Using the full powers of her newly-found resolve, she maintained the focus there until her entire physical body vanished from awareness, and her mind went absolutely still. Withdrawing slightly from deep samādhi, she immediately saw another vision. This time the vision was a portent of Dhamma. Opening her inner eye, she saw Ajaan Mahā Boowa walking toward her, carrying in his hand a radiant, razor-sharp knife. Pointing the knife directly at her body, he announced that he was going to demonstrate the proper way to investigate the physical body. With that, he began to methodically chop her body to pieces. Slashing repeatedly with the sharp knife, he dismembered her whole body, cutting it into smaller and smaller fragments.

Mae Chee Kaew stared transfixed as body parts fell to the ground around her. She watched as Ajaan Mahā Boowa dissected each part further until nothing remained of her body except a disjointed heap of flesh, bones and sinews. Addressing her internal awareness, Ajaan Mahā Boowa asked, "Which piece is a person? Look at them all — compare them. Which piece is a woman? Which is a man? Which one is attractive? Which one is desirable?"

At that point, she was faced with a bloody mess of body parts. They were so disgusting in nature that she was totally dismayed to think she had clung to them for so long. She continued watching as the remains of her body were scattered about until, finally, nothing remained. At that moment, her mind felt drawn back inside, and the flow of her consciousness decisively reversed direction, dropping to the base of samādhi, and converging to the very center of her being. Only a simple and harmonious awareness remained, alone on its own. The knowing essence of mind was so exceedingly refined as to be indescribable. It simply knew — a profoundly subtle state of inner awareness pervaded.

By decisively reversing her focus inward, Mae Chee Kaew halted the normal flow of consciousness and realized the true essence of mind — the very essence or source of awareness. Within the heart's central chamber, she experienced an ungraspable sense of vast space, beyond measure — the wondrous nature of the formless essence of awareness. When focusing inward, she suddenly forgot the focusing, and entered utter quiescence. Not a single thought arose. Everything was empty silence. Body and mind were in a state of great freedom, and all objects — including her body — disappeared without a trace. Utterly tranquil, her mind stayed for many hours bathed in its own solitude.

As soon as her mind began withdrawing from deep samādhi, she detected a subtle movement of consciousness — almost imperceptible, at first — as it started to flow out from the mind's essence, and move away from the center. As the momentum of consciousness grew, she clearly observed a strong and immediate urge for the mind to turn its attention outward, in the direction of external perceptions. The tendency was so much a part of her nature that she had hardly noticed it before. Suddenly, this conscious outflow stood out clearly against the background of the serene tranquility of the mind's true essence. In order to reverse the normal course of consciousness and keep her awareness firmly centered inside, she was forced to put up a mighty struggle against its out-flowing inclination. She thought of Ajaan Mahā Boowa and reflected on his severe admonitions. Now certain that he was right, she renewed her resolve to rein in her mind's wayward tendencies.

During the next several days, Mae Chee Kaew concentrated on finding a reliable method for firmly anchoring her awareness inside. Emerging from deep samādhi, she clearly comprehended the challenge of controlling the mind's outward flow, and refused to allow its impulsive movement to take over and drag away her attention. The mind's out-flowing movement was always accompanied by the activities of thought and imagination. That flowing, revolving consciousness created and maintained the entire sentient universe. But when not a single thought arose, spontaneous mindfulness was born. Being a moment of pure attention, this awareness of the present was alert, but relaxed. It did not fall into the elements of body and mind, where material and spiritual illusions took charge. In the past, upon withdrawing from samādhi, all sorts of images appeared in her awareness for no apparent reason, enticing her mind in their direction. She felt she could not turn them away if she wanted to, and even felt comfortable going along with them. When the mind stayed unified until pure mindfulness arose, she witnessed the moment-to-moment creation and cessation of a myriad of thoughts and images, while remaining detached and dispassionate. Having witnessed the essential transformation of focused awareness, she realized the value of receiving the guidance of a true teacher.

When she felt confident that she could effectively reverse her mind's dynamic flow, by unifying it and keeping it grounded in the present, she decided to risk Ajaan Mahā Boowa's displeasure and return to Nok An Cave, so she could respectfully relate her progress in meditation. When she arrived at the cave, she was met by Ajaan Mahā Boowa's stern, unwelcoming countenance.

"Why have you come again?" he barked. "I told you to stay away! This is no place for a great sage!"

She pleaded with him to let her speak, to listen to what she had to say. She explained that the traumatic experience of being chased away had caused her to accept her faults and take seriously his advice to focus inward. In precise detail, she described the new direction of her meditation, and how she had learned to maintain detached presence of mind. She knew she had been wrong to value her mis-guided knowledge of spiritual phenomena, which she now realized had gotten her nowhere. She had worked hard for several days dis-covering how to control her mind's dynamic tendencies, until she finally succeeded in keeping it solidly centered inside. With immense gratitude, and a sense of accomplishment, she had returned to pay homage to her teacher, and humbly ask for his forgiveness.

Only those who practice meditation can truly understand the spiritual path. But learning meditation properly requires the guid-ance of a gifted teacher. The teacher cannot afford to make even the slightest mistake, especially when his disciple is meditating at a very high level. The teacher must know more than the disciple, so that she can respectfully follow his lead. It is wrong for a teacher to teach above his level of understanding. The disciple will not benefit from such instruction. When a teaching is based on direct experience of the truth, gained through penetrating insight, a talented disciple will be able to progress very quickly along the path of wisdom.

Seeing that her meditation was now firmly on the right path, Ajaan Mahā Boowa graciously accepted her back. He told her that she had been living with the ghosts of her mind for too long. Compulsively following the flow of her conscious mind had caused her to live at the mercy of ghosts and spirits, and to be a slave to the phantoms created by her own mind. By turning the flow of consciousness back on itself, she temporarily interrupted its momentum, and restored the mind to its essence. What she experienced was the true essence of mind — the mind's intrinsic knowing nature. Consciousness is a function of the mind's essence, but conscious activity is transient and lacks the mind's intrinsic quality of awareness. States of consciousness exist in conjunction with the awareness that knows them, and the knowing essence of mind is the very root and source of that awareness. The transient states of mind that arise and cease within the flow of consciousness are merely conditioned phenomena. Because the mind's essence is conditioned by nothing, it is the only stable reality.

Consciousness naturally flows out from the mind's essence, moving from the center of the mind to the surface. Surface consciousness constantly changes form, shape and substance as it is rippled by the shifting winds of greed, anger and delusion. But the true essence of mind exhibits no activities and manifests no conditions. Being pure awareness, it simply knows. The activities that spring from mind essence, such as awareness of the material world or the spiritual world, are conditions of the consciousness that emanates from the mind. Since consciousness represents mental activities and conditions that are, by their very nature, constantly arising and ceasing, conscious awareness is always unstable and unreliable.

When the outward flow of consciousness intersects with the perceptual fields of the sensory organs, awareness becomes mixed up with the objects of its perception. When consciousness intersects with the eyes, sight conditions consciousness, and consciousness becomes seeing. When consciousness intersects with the ears, sound conditions consciousness, and consciousness becomes hearing, and so forth. Therefore when sense consciousness arises, the essence of mind is obscured and cannot be found. It is not that the essence has disappeared, but that its knowing nature has been transmuted into consciousness. Ordinarily, when people allow their eyes and ears to pursue sights and sounds, they become emotionally involved with what they perceive, calming down only when those sense objects are gone. Becoming obsessed with the endless parade of ghosts and spirits in the ordinary conscious mind, they completely miss the mind's true essence.

By reversing the flow of consciousness, thoughts are interrupted and brought to a halt. When thought ceases, consciousness converges inside, merging into the mind's knowing essence. With persistent practice, this foundation becomes unshakable in all circumstances. Then, even when the mind withdraws from deep samādhi, it still feels solid and compact, as though nothing can disturb the mind's inward focus. While samādhi does not bring an end to suffering, it does constitute an ideal platform from which to launch an all out assault on the mental defilements that cause suffering. Observation becomes spontaneous and instinctive, and mindfulness remains fully present. This sharp and immediate focus complements the investigative and contemplative work of wisdom. The profound calm and concentration generated by samādhi becomes an excellent basis for the development of penetrative insight into the nature of existence.

There are two main objectives for bringing thought to a halt. One is to open up space to clarify the nature of thought, by distinguishing compulsive and habitual thinking from deliberate and focused thinking. The other is to clear room for the conscious operation of non-conceptual insight. Both are indispensible aspects of wisdom. Properly practiced, samādhi can stop thought temporarily, but it does not distort reason. It enables one to think deliberately rather than compulsively. This use of mind opens a wider space for thought with the ability to think and observe with detached clarity. Direct perception can see at a glance where a train of thought will lead. Using independent and intuitive insight, one can put down useless thoughts and take up useful ones, thus building a firm basis for transcendent wisdom. As long as the mind has not reached supreme quiet, it cannot properly think. Thinking caused by the ongoing momentum of consciousness is random thinking, not essential thinking. Knowledge gained from conceptual thought is superficial and unreliable. It lacks the essential insight of true wisdom.

A mind undistracted by peripheral thoughts and emotions focuses exclusively on its field of awareness, and investigates the phenomena arising there in the light of truth, without interference from guesswork or speculation. This is an important principle. The investigation proceeds smoothly, with fluency and skill. Never distracted or misled by conjecture, genuine wisdom investigates, contemplates and understands at a deeply profound level.

Because Mae Chee Kaew had been bound up with the products of consciousness for so long, and thus alienated from its essence, it was necessary for her to directly experience the mind's true essence. But experiencing the essence was a means rather than an end — a means of freeing the mind from gross mental hindrances, and laying a solid foundation for further development. Ajaan Mahā Boowa warned her that the experience of mind essence could easily lead her to a false sense of confidence in the knowledge arising from concious perceptions. This made it imperative that everything flowing from the mind be investigated carefully. Each time that she withdrew from deep samādhi, it was necessary to examine the activities of consciousness for the remaining taints of compulsive mental conditioning, ruled by lingering attachments to physical form, mental imagery and thought formation.

In this way, Ajaan Mahā Boowa taught Mae Chee Kaew how to probe deeper into her mind so that she could learn to completely uproot the mental defilements that were wrapped tightly around her heart. He reiterated that this — and not the perception of countless phenomena in the conventional world — was the essence of Buddhist practice. He urged her to first turn her mental energy toward solving the enigma of physical embodiment, and the mind's inevitable attachment to form. He reminded her that the practice of wisdom begins with the human body, the objective being to directly penetrate the body's true nature.

In investigating the body, he taught her to make use of the power of spontaneous observation as a contemplative technique. So as to avoid falling into conditioned patterns of thinking — based on habitual interpretations and fueled by conjecture and supposition — Mae Chee Kaew must employ the clear, unclouded mindfulness present right where consciousness emerged from the mind's true essence. For spontaneous insight to arise, the limitations of ordinary thinking and imagining must be overcome. That meant perceiving the objects of investigation just as they appeared in her mind, all at once without conceptualizing. If she allowed the conscious mind to discriminate, by naming and labeling mental formations, then normal mundane conditioning would generate a proliferation of thought, and lead to profuse confusion — the very antithesis of true insight. By spontaneously observing phenomena with clear mindfulness, she could develop a sense of freedom from the things she perceived, and attain wisdom's natural, unobstructed clarity.

Seeing the suffering caused by attachment to one's body is the initial insight that focuses the mind on Dhamma. Those who see the body clearly tend to understand Dhamma quickly.

The Corpse Within

Walking back to nunnery that evening, Mae Chee Kaew felt wondrously bright and buoyant in both body and mind. Reaching her small hut just as dusk fell, she seated herself in meditation as usual and comprehensively reviewed her meditation practice. Samādhi attainments had always come easily to Mae Chee Kaew; her mind tended naturally toward integration. Only a well-integrated mind could attain the kind of access concentration needed to directly experience the vast world of spiritual energies she encountered so readily. When her flow of consciousness converged to its natural center, it touched base with the true essence of mind, but only briefly, before rebounding out to resume its normal dynamics. That brief experience of mind essence led to a mistaken sense of certainty about the knowledge arising from her subsequent perceptions.

Rather than using that calm and concentrated mental focus to examine those transient states of mind, Mae Chee Kaew passively watched her mind's changing panorama, letting her faculties of thought and imagination speculate on the meaning of what occurred there. Since the conclusions reached by conceptual thought are superficial and personal, she had lost touch with the detached awareness of the mind's essence, thereby falling victim to corrosive elements of consciousness that gave an emotional bias to her perceptions, and led her astray from genuine understanding. Her conscious mind became so involved with its habitual fabrications that it appeared to have an independent existence from its original essence.

Ajaan Mahā Boowa's dramatic intervention changed that. Now, when her flow of consciousness converged to its natural center, it reunited with the mind's essence, completely merging into the wondrous nature of pure awareness, and resting totally in supreme tranquility. Body and consciousness vanished. An indescribably subtle awareness was the only thing to remain. There was no movement, not even the slightest rippling of consciousness. Only after her mind remained immersed in tranquility for a sufficient time did it stir and begin to withdraw from the center. A brief ripple of consciousness occurred, and then quickly disappeared. The rippling happened naturally of its own accord; it was not intended. A slight movement, immediately followed by stillness. Conscious moments surfaced and vanished many times, gradually increasing in frequency until the flow of consciousness eventually reestablished its normal momentum.

Although she had regained awareness of her external environment, the conceptual faculties of her mind remained dormant. Her consciousness was suspended in a fluid and spontaneous state of awareness where the knowing nature of the essence continued to overrule the mind's normal thinking patterns. Due to this spontaneity, unbounded awareness and specific perception were functioning at the same time, allowing her to understand her mind and body at a deeply intuitive level of insight. She knew instinctively that she must hold her attention at that level when examining phenomena in order to attain the penetrative insights of true wisdom. Wisdom was able to function effectively within the normal flow of consciousness, because her habitual thinking patterns no longer prevented access to deeper spontaneous knowledge gained through direct intuition by a more subtle faculty of knowing.

Emerging from the deep tranquility of samādhi late that night, Mae Chee Kaew experienced the flow of her consciousness spreading out slowly through every part of her body until she perceived its entire form all at once. Preconceptions about the body did not intrude on her awareness. She simply concentrated on the form of her body as it actually was, in a sitting position. Her detached awareness knew intuitively that inherent within her bodily form was a process of continuous decay that eventually culminated in the body's death and disintegration. With a profound degree of mental clarity, she picked up the thread of her body's ongoing decay and began to follow that natural course to its inevitable conclusion. The process of decay started deep within the inner cavities of her body and slowly spread throughout every part. She simply observed, without thinking or imagining, and allowed her body's breakup to unfold within the field of her awareness. Soon the natural course of decay for a dead body assumed a spontaneous momentum all its own.

Beginning at the head, Mae Chee Kaew let her attention gradually filter down through the whole corpse, allowing the images of decay to become sharp and clear. Because her intuitive wisdom had become fully attuned in the notion of death and disintegration, spontaneous changes began occurring in the flowing imagery. She felt her inner corpse begin to swell and slowly change color, the skin turning yellow, then molting into bluish-black. As the body swelled, the skin stretched taut, then ruptured and peeled back, revealing rotting flesh and oozing fluids that quickly attracted a swarm of flies. Gradually the stench of rotting flesh became nauseating, and nearly unbearable to her internal senses. The flies laid eggs, and maggots appeared, spreading out and moving as a writhing mass, in and around the ruptures of peeling skin and oozing flesh, to eventually cover the whole corpse. By the time the maggots had eaten their fill of rotten tissue, most of the flesh and internal organs were gone. Without the connective tissue, the skeleton fell apart and slumped over in a pile, leaving a heap of filthy bones, streaked with remnants of decaying flesh and bound together with twisted strands of tendon and cartilage. Further disintegration left the bones disjointed, and scattered, the skeleton contorted.

With the passage of time, rain and weather, the residual bits of flesh and tendon were washed away, leaving only bones bleached milky white by the sun. Eventually, the bones too began to breakup and disintegrate, until only the larger chunks remained in a disordered heap; the skull in one place, the pelvis in another. Finally, even these pieces were worn away, swallowed up and reclaimed by the earth element from which they originated. Suddenly, the earth itself vanished, leaving nothing but pure, crystal-clear awareness radiating out in all directions. Gradually, the sense of being in the midst of radiant awareness disappeared, taking with it all sense of self, and of the environment.

Mae Chee Kaew meditated in that way every day. She focused on the corpse within over and over again until the experience of death and decay became habitual features of her mind's conscious perspective, and the mental image of her body began to decompose every time she turned her attention to it. In each meditation sitting, Mae Chee Kaew's inner eye watched the process of dissolution unfold with a deepening sense of calm and clarity. Gradually, the constant breakup of bodily substance drew her attention to the body's fragmentary nature, so she began concentrating on its constituent elements — the properties of earth, water, fire and wind that comprise all matter. Flesh, bones, teeth, nails and hair had the solid material characteristics of earth. Blood, urine, mucus and other fluid secretions possessed the liquid qualities of water. Fire was present as warmth, energy and vitality in the body. The wind element was evident in breathing, circulation and bodily movement.

Mae Chee Kaew observed how decay broke down the material bonds that hold elements together within the body, and how it released them to revert to their original, elemental state. The occurrence of death, when consciousness abandoned the body for good, released the life-giving forces of fire and wind to return to their elemental conditions. Observing further, from the inner perspective of spontaneous awareness, she watched as bodily liquids seeped into the ground, or evaporated into the air. When the liquid elements had either drained into the ground or vanished into the air, the bodily parts dried out, gradually dehydrating until only hardened tissue and bare bones remained. Slowly crumbling, and then turning to dust, those parts finally returned completely to the earth element.

Mae Chee Kaew vividly observed bones merging with earth, the two coalescing together to become one and the same substance. When the last residue of bone returned to its original, elemental state, her heart became absorbed in the profound realization of the body's insubstantial and illusory nature. Knowledge and understanding arose that all bodily substance is a combination of earth, water, fire and wind, and that they had all returned to their original elemental state. Suddenly, the earth itself disappeared from awareness, leaving her perception filled with bright light, radiating in all directions. Then, in a flash, her awareness plunged to a level of integration she had never experienced before. With that, the radiant light vanished. An indescribable emptiness remained — a state of absolute oneness, without a single moment of duality. There was only pure awareness — a transcendent and marvelous state of perfect tranquility, totally devoid of distinguishing characteristics — the vibrant emptiness of the mind's true essence.

The elemental transformation of the body into earth, water, fire and wind was vividly distinct every time Mae Chee Kaew investigated it. She saw clearly that nothing dies. Hair, nails, teeth, skin, flesh, bones: reduced to their original elemental form, they are simply the earth element. Since when did the earth element ever die? When they decomposed and disintegrated, what did they become? All bodily matter reverted to its original properties. The earth and water elements reclaimed their original properties, as did the wind and fire elements. Nothing was destroyed. Those elements simply came together to form a mass in which the conscious mind took up residence. The mind attached itself to the mass of matter and animated it, then carried it as a burden by building a self-identity around it.

By laying personal claim to the physical body, the mind acquired endless amounts of pain and suffering.

The mind never died, either. At most there was constant change, birth and death arising and passing in every conscious moment, following one another in an endless continuum. The more fully Mae Chee Kaew investigated the four elements, observing them disintegrate into their original properties, the more distinctly pronounced the mind appeared. So where was death to be found? And what was it that died? The four elements — earth, water, fire and wind — they did not die. As for the mind, how could it die? With this understanding, her mind became more conspicuous, more aware and more insightful.

Withdrawing from supreme tranquility, Mae Chee Kaew contemplated the profound and far-reaching implications of physical embodiment. She realized that her sense of body was one domain of self-identity. From birth, she had always organized the world around bodily perceptions, being instinctively preoccupied with the protection of the body, and the fulfillment of its material appetites. She clearly discerned that thoughts formed on the basis of the body were karmic causes keeping her continually bound to the cycle of birth and death. The body's innate impurity actually went much deeper than its physical form. It extended to many bodily based attitudes and actions that were not only repulsive, but very damaging. Vanity, sensual obsessions, sexual aggression and physical violence were ugliness of a much more insidious type. Being responsible for such a large array of negative thoughts and emotions, identification with bodily form connected the mind to the root of saṁsāric existence. She realized that if she wanted to trace bodily attachment to its source, she would have to directly investigate those defiling thoughts and emotions, and the flow of consciousness that spawned them.

In a perfectly still and crystal-clear pool of water, we can see everything with clarity. The heart at complete rest is still. When the heart is still, wisdom appears easily, fluently. When wisdom flows, clear understanding follows.

Spontaneous Awareness

Months passed by as Mae Chee Kaew's life settled into a quiet and steady passage centered on the rigors of intensive meditation. Retiring to the seclusion of her hut shortly after the morning meal, she spent the morning hours pacing her meditation path from end to end. The meditation path had become a sacred battleground for Mae Chee Kaew in her struggle to vanquish the cycle of birth and death. She paced its length with an inward focus so complete that she was unaware of her body's position or of her bare feet touching the earth. Her awareness was so internalized that occasionally her body veered off the walking surface and into the undergrowth. Without losing concentration, she instinctively steered herself back to the path and resumed walking, her attention resolutely fixed on the flowing current of consciousness.

The path was shaded by a leafy canopy of towering hardwoods and arching bamboo. At one end stood a tall and slender *phayom* tree under whose shade Mae Chee Kaew had built a rustic bamboo platform where she could rest and meditate during the hot midday hours. The *phayom* tree, a variety of rainforest mahogany, had become one of her favorite spots. The *phayom* was a steely and compact wood that was admired for its bright yellow blossoms, which dotted the green foliage during seasonal bursts and littered her small meditation platform with its falling petals. Combining hardness and beauty, the *phayom* was indicative of the toughness and splendor that characterized Mae Chee Kaew's present state of mind.

Late one evening Mae Chee Kaew had a vision. The vista of a spacious pool filled with golden lotus blossoms stretched before her mind's eye. The floating blossoms were as big as oxcart wheels, their thin, fine gold petals flaring like feathery spokes. Other lotus flowers, their petals closed around the stem and pointing skyward, stood tall above the azure water like gold-domed temples. Others were submerged just below the surface of the clear cool water, their radiance rippling across the pool like a golden breeze. The water appeared so magically transparent that the soft undulating mud on the bottom was clearly visible. Detached from their stems, some of the petals floated on the surface, wet and sparkling, their delicate fragrance permeating the air in all directions. As Mae Chee Kaew watched in quiet awe, a small golden duck glided down from the sky, skimmed across the placid surface and began swimming playfully among the lotus blossoms. It pecked at the floating petals, gracefully circling each petal as it ate. After consuming four petals it stopped, satisfied, and remained perfectly still. Watching, fascinated, from the edge of the lotus pond, Mae Chee Kaew felt her body lift and float, like a cloud, over the water. As she approached the golden duck, she felt her legs spread to straddle its back. But as she mounted, she merged completely with it. At that instant she realized that she herself was the golden duck. Immediately she withdrew from samādhi meditation and returned to normal consciousness.

Mae Chee Kaew thought about this mystical vision for days, searching for its essential meaning. A gold duck eating golden lotus blossoms. Lotus flowers symbolize offerings in homage to the Dhamma, the essence of the Buddha's noble path. Gold stands for light, the light of the mind; the flower represents the blossoming, or opening up, of the mind's radiant light. She understood that the four lotus petals were the four *ariya magga*, the four milestones on the noble path to arahantship. Like the golden duck, Mae Chee Kaew radiated the clear, luminous light of understanding: knowledge that in this lifetime she would surely complete her journey along that noble path.

Mae Chee Kaew knew that consciousness pervaded all moments of awareness, regardless of whether attention was focused internally or externally. Nothing she experienced ever stood outside consciousness. Since all phenomena were grasped, conceived and experienced only on that basis, they had no independent existence separate from the conscious mind. For that reason, awareness of the body was inherently a function of consciousness. In essence, she was investigating an internalized bodily form, a mental picture of the body based on sensation. Consciousness spread out naturally through the entire body, animating the sense spheres and activating sensory awareness. The experience of embodiment — of body as self — was comprised chiefly of mental images shaped in conjunction with sensory awareness of her body, and colored by a deep-rooted attachment to form and personal identity.

With a sense of spontaneity and detachment, Mae Chee Kaew focused on the body as a mental construct, as a product of the conscious mind. If the physical body was merely a conglomeration of elements, temporarily lumped together, where did the sense of embodiment come from? And what initiated thoughts of ugliness, or emotions of revulsion, in response to the natural process of bodily decay and disintegration?

As she focused on internalized images of the body's dissolution, Mae Chee Kaew paid particular attention to the accompanying thoughts and emotions that defined their appearance as either agreeable or disagreeable. Becoming a detached and unbiased witness, she gave the discriminating mind free rein to first conceptualize, and then react to its interpretations. She knew her body only through feedback from the senses, combined with the mind's conceptual activity. But she then experienced those sensual concepts as being either positive and good, or negative and bad. She needed to understand why the mind created those images, and how the mind suffused them with meaning.

At this stage, Mae Chee Kaew began to focus exclusively on the emotional responses evoked by body contemplation. She had become adept at interrupting the mind's conscious momentum, and reversing its normal course back to the source. So, she started to use the same technique to reverse the flood of thought and emotion, and retrace its course to the point of origin. She concentrated on an image of advanced bodily decay, absorbing it all at once without conceptualization. With spontaneous awareness and specific perception functioning together, she noticed an instinctive surge of revulsion push its way out from deep inside her to permeate the image. She held the image in her awareness until object and observer became one. At that moment, image and emotion gradually contracted and drew inward until both were fully absorbed by the conscious mind. Then they simply vanished. Quickly she refocused on the mental image and its attached sense of revulsion; and again, watched as the flow of mental perception, infusing the image with emotional impact, reverted to its source, merging with the center of consciousness and then disappearing. The more she focused in that way, the more spontaneous the reversal of image and emotion became. Eventually, on their own, without prompting, images and emotions receded into the mind, returning to their original source, where they vanished immediately.

Mae Chee Kaew's meditation had reached a decisive phase in body contemplation, a turning point in which the root-cause of the mind's attachment to bodily form was seen in stark clarity. As instinctive feelings of revulsion reunited with their primary cause, a profound realization suddenly occurred: the mind itself produced feelings of revulsion and attraction; the mind alone created perceptions of ugliness and beauty. Those qualities did not actually exist in the objects of perception. The mind projected those attributes onto the images it perceived, and then deceived itself into believing that the objects themselves were beautiful and attractive, or ugly and repulsive. In truth, the flow of consciousness was consistently steeped in a proliferation of mental imagery and attending emotion. Her mind painted elaborate pictures all the time — pictures of herself and pictures of the external world. It then fell for its own mental imagery, believing it to be substantially real.

At that stage, the infinite, space-like awareness of mind essence and the particularity of conscious perception were operating simultaneously. Gradually the illusion of cohesive mental images began to break down as well. Within the flowing current of consciousness, myriad amorphous forms and fragmentary shapes arose, coalesced into images, and then broke apart immediately, only to regroup and disband time and time again. No sooner did an image of the body appear than it vanished instantly. Before a particular desire or expression could fully formulate, the source of awareness simply enveloped it, causing it to dissolve into emptiness and disappear. Countless potential ways in which body and mind could express themselves seemed to arise in random succession, only to dissolve into emptiness, one after another. Habitual concepts of bodily existence expressed a desire to take form and declare their individual characteristics, but the knowing essence dissolved them all before they could establish a definite presence in the mind.

Rising and passing images happened so quickly that concepts of external and internal were no longer relevant. In the end, forms flickered on and off, appearing and disappearing from consciousness in such rapid succession that their meaning was no longer discernable. After each disappearance, awareness experienced profound emptiness — emptiness of imagery, and emptiness of attachment to form. An extremely refined essence of pure knowing stood out within the mind. As each new image flashed and vanished, the mind felt the resulting emptiness more profoundly. From that point on, Mae Chee Kaew's mind was wondrously empty and clear. Even though the body remained, her awareness was empty. No image of any sort remained within the mind.

This insight occasioned a momentous revolution of Mae Chee Kaew's entire being. She understood the truth with absolute certainty: delusion about imagery produced by the flow of consciousness leads to feelings of repulsion and attraction. She realized that both were rooted in a deeply instinctive, but almost subliminal, distortion of conscious perceptions of body and form. When the real basis of those perceptions was exposed, completely undermining their validity, the external world of appearances collapsed, and her attachment to it ceased of its own accord. With the cessation of all images created by the mind, came the cessation of attachment to form. Once her mind had withdrawn completely from all sensual involvement, a feeling of profound serenity enveloped her entire mental being.

Finally, for Mae Chee Kaew, bodily images, even as bare forms, no longer existed within her mind's conscious framework. Since no shapes or forms remained in the mind to be grasped, Mae Chee Kaew knew she could never be reborn in the realms of form again. The mind's usual sense of physical limitation and embodiment completely disappeared. She felt her being dissolve, expand outward and merge with all things, as though forming one essence with the universe; resting within, unfettered by any dependency, was a supreme emptiness — clear, bright and still.

Purity is the mind's normal state. It becomes blemished only because it accepts external intrusions, which make emotions like sadness and joy arise and proliferate until the mind becomes totally blinded to its own true nature.

Luminous Essence

The hut, the meditation path and the little platform under the *phayom* tree were Mae Chee Kaew's constant companions throughout the year. Except for her daily meal, she seldom left the confines of her meditation environment. Although the nuns still went to see Ajaan Mahā Boowa once a week on lunar observance days, Mae Chee Kaew rarely accompanied them, instead choosing to focus on intensifying her meditation practice. Despite Mae Chee Kaew's dedication to her practice, she still possessed an abiding sense of gratitude and respect for Ajaan Mahā Boowa and so every morning she cooked a small pot of sticky rice and prepared a basket of betel nut for him. Normally, Mae Chee Kaew would have one of the nuns bring her daily offering to Ajaan Mahā Boowa, only occasionally did she go herself; and even then she would speak with him only briefly.

Ajaan Mahā Boowa's monastery was situated northeast of town, while Mae Chee Kaew's nunnery was two miles away to the southwest. Baan Huay Sai was in the middle. Despite the distance and the fact that he never announced his travel plans in advance, Mae Chee Kaew always knew intuitively when Ajaan Mahā Boowa left his monastery to wander through the region in search of solitude. She always knew when he had vacated his monastery, and she always knew when his return was imminent. Mae Chee Kaew said she would suddenly feel a chill pervade the environment when Ajaan Mahā Boowa went away. And although he often traveled for months, Mae Chee Kaew always knew when he was coming as she could feel the warmth returning even before he arrived. The chill and the warmth were the external signs that came through perception; but the knowing came from inside her heart.

As soon as Ajaan Mahā Boowa left to wander, Mae Chee Kaew immediately told the nuns not to cook the pot of sticky rice or prepare the basket of betel nut. Several months later, when she sensed his return, she would tell the nuns to begin cooking the rice and preparing the betel nut for him once again. Normally, when he was living at the monastery, the nuns prepared only sticky rice for him. But on the day of his return, Mae Chee Kaew insisted that the nuns prepare fluffy rice as a special offering. On the morning after his return, the nuns appeared at the monastery bearing gifts of rice and betel nut. He asked the nuns how they knew he was back in the monastery since he had only arrived late the evening before. The nuns replied that Mae Chee Kaew had sensed his return and therefore asked them to prepare the usual offerings. Each time he returned from these travels, Ajaan Mahā Boowa heard the same thing. Mae Chee Kaew always knew; she never failed.

Mae Chee Kaew had learned to examine phenomena using the specific perceptions of consciousness in tandem with the expansive awareness of intrinsic mental essence. She realized that consciousness flowed naturally from the mind essence to initiate perceptual activity. And perceptions were defined and interpreted by the mind's conceptual movement, which had its origin in the motionless essence. So she focused exclusively on the moment that the conscious flow stirred and emerged from the stillness of her mind's vital center.

Each thought, each spark of an idea, ripples briefly through the mind, then ceases. Individually, these mental ripples have no specific meaning. They merely flash briefly into awareness and then disappear without a trace. Fragmentary ideas — the elements of thought — flash on and off with distinct beginnings and endings, like flashes of lightning or the blinking of fireflies. But the mental recognition that interprets their significance disperses more slowly through the mind, blanketing the flowing consciousness like a moving fog, before coalescing into distinct conceptual forms. Together, memories and thoughts combine to conjure up the concepts and notions of personal existence.

Conceptual activity consists of naturally occurring mental phenomena that arise and cease spontaneously. These phenomena possess no awareness of their own. The awareness that knows them is the mind essence, the knowing nature that permeates everything. The mind is basically non-dual; it is just one vital reality. The flow of consciousness from the knowing center creates the illusion of duality, of inside and outside, of knower and known.

Forms and concepts are phenomena conditioned by the movement of consciousness. Because of a subtle and pervasive delusion existing in the minds of all beings, the awareness that knows forms and concepts becomes attached to these creations of consciousness. Grasping at an individual, personal identity, the mind turns feelings, memories and thoughts into self. That grasping turns the mind itself into a personality. But thinking and feeling are actually just condition-ed functions of the mind; not its original essence. Essence turning into consciousness creates a conceptual reality, not an essential one. And the conceptual reality of self is the object of deep-seated attach-ment.

Mae Chee Kaew realized that the true mind had no form, and formed no conceptions. By spontaneously observing phenomena with clear mindfulness, she attained freedom from conceptual thinking, which allowed the knowing essence to relinquish mental constructs before they could establish a definite presence in the mind's conscious continuum. Before a particular thought or expression could fully form, the knowing essence simply let go, causing mental formations to dissolve into nothingness. Eventually, the detached nature of the mind's true essence became so all-encompassing that the multitude of conscious expressions failed to take hold, dissolving before its still, potent immanence.

At that stage, Mae Chee Kaew's mind resembled a battlefield where the forces of conscious existence were pitted against the all-embracing essence, which encompassed everything, but retained noth-ing. As profound emptiness constantly dissolved countless forms of emerging existence, the mind's knowing essence gained the upper hand, increasing in brightness and purity.

When insight thoroughly penetrated the illusory nature of men-tal phenomena, the knowing essence relinquished all concepts, fully recognizing that they were merely ripples inside the mind and had no real substance. No matter how they appeared mentally, they were just conditioned forms — conventions of the mind that simply vanished into emptiness. There were no exceptions.

Mae Chee Kaew's meditation was destroying mental patterns that have dominated saṁsāric existence for eons. Not a single thought managed to rise or form, indicating that true, spontaneous mindfulness was born. The mind's spontaneous observation was pure, undiluted attention, that led naturally to clear and penetrating insight. When the mind understands clearly with intuitive wisdom that no self can be found within mental phenomena, liberating detachment occurs of its own accord. As the mind's focus grows narrower, the currents sent out by the mind grow shorter and more limited. Mae Chee Kaew had investigated and understood conceptual phenomena so thoroughly that the clear, bright essence no longer made conscious contact with them. Thought and imagination within the mind had come to a complete halt. The mind's essential knowing nature stood out alone, on its own.

Except for an exceedingly refined awareness — an awareness that suffused the entire cosmos — absolutely nothing appeared. Mind transcended conditions of time and space. A luminous essence of being that seemed boundless, yet wondrously empty, permeated everything throughout the universe. Everything seemed to be filled by a subtle quality of knowing, as if nothing else existed. Cleansed of the things that clouded and obscured its all-encompassing essence, her mind revealed its true power.

When the offshoots of delusion were completely cut, her mind converged into a nucleus of sublime radiance — a radiance so majestic and mesmerizing that Mae Chee Kaew felt certain it signaled the end of all suffering that she had been striving to attain. Having relinquished all attachment to the factors of personal identity, the subtle radiant splendor at the center of the mind became her sole remaining focus. The focal point of her awareness was so exceedingly delicate and refined as to be indescribable, and emitted a happiness that was unprecedented and so wondrous that it seemed to entirely transcend the realm of conditioned phenomena. The luminous mind exuded a strong sense of power and invulnerability. Nothing seemed capable of affecting it. Mae Chee Kaew was now certain that she had finally reached the ultimate goal, Nibbāna.

Seeing delusion clearly in a flash of insight,
we become fed up with our attachment to this
mass of suffering and loosen our grip. In that
moment of coolness, the fires in our heart abate,
and freedom from suffering arises naturally of
its own accord.

Phayom in Full Bloom

By the middle of October 1952 the *phayom* tree was in full and
radiant bloom. Sitting beneath it one afternoon, her mind awash in
splendor, Mae Chee Kaew felt the time was right to inform Ajaan
Mahā Boowa about her crowning achievement. He was, after all, the
inspiration that had led her to this profound majestic radiance of
mind. It was time she repaid his confidence in her with the fruits
of her triumph. As it was a lunar observance day, she went to visit
him late in the afternoon. She left the nunnery with several nuns as
companions, walking together through the fields that rimmed the
village until they reached the other side. From there they began the
steep climb to Ajaan Mahā Boowa's mountain cave.

Seeing Ajaan Mahā Boowa seated at the cave's entrance, Mae Chee
Kaew prostrated before her teacher to pay obeisance and exchanged
greetings with him. She then bowed her head, pressed her palms
together and asked permission to speak. She spoke of her progress

over the past year, carefully detailing the consecutive stages of her experience, and concluded with her "lion's roar", the radiant emptiness of mind that permeated the entire cosmos and transcended all conditions.

When she stopped speaking, Ajaan Mahā Boowa looked up and calmly asked, "Is that all?" Mae Chee Kaew nodded. Ajaan Mahā Boowa paused for a moment and then spoke:

> "When you investigate mental phenomena until you go be-
> yond them completely, the remaining defiling elements of
> consciousness will be drawn into a radiant nucleus of aware-
> ness, which merges with the mind's naturally radiant essence.
> This radiance is so majestic and mesmerizing that even tran-
> scendent faculties like spontaneous mindfulness and intuitive
> wisdom invariably fall under its spell. The mind's brightness
> and clarity appear to be so extraordinary and awe-inspiring,
> that nothing can possibly compare. The luminous essence
> is the epitome of perfect goodness and virtue, the ultimate
> in spiritual happiness. It is your true, original self — the
> core of your being. But this true self is also the fundamental
> source of all attachment to being and becoming. Ultimately
> it is attachment to the allure of this primordial radiance of
> mind that causes living beings to wander indefinitely through
> the world of becoming and ceasing, constantly grasping at
> birth and enduring death.
>
> "The fundamental cause of that attachment is the very
> delusion about your true self. Delusion is responsible for
> all the defiling elements of consciousness, and its avenue

of escape is the ongoing momentum of conscious activity. In this sphere, delusion reigns supreme. But once mindfulness and wisdom are skilled enough to eliminate conscious activity and therefore close this outlet, delusions created by the flow of mental phenomena cease. Severing all of its external outflows leaves delusion no room to maneuver inside the mind, forcing it to gather into the radiant nucleus from which all knowing emanates. That center of knowing appears as a luminous emptiness that truly overwhelms and amazes.

"But that radiant emptiness should not be mistaken for the pure emptiness of Nibbāna. The two are as different as night and day. The radiant mind is the original mind of the cycle of constant becoming; but it is not the essence of mind which is fully pure and free from birth and death. Radiance is a very subtle, natural condition whose uniform brightness and clarity make it appear empty. This is your original nature beyond name and form. But it is not yet Nibbāna. It is the very substance of mind that has been well-cleansed to the point where a mesmerizing and majestic quality of knowing is its outstanding feature. When the mind finally relinquishes all attachment to forms and concepts, the knowing essence assumes exceedingly refined qualities. It has let go of everything — except itself. It remains permeated by a fundamental delusion about its own true nature. Because of that, the radiant essence has turned into a subtle form of self without you realizing it. You end up believing that the subtle feelings of happiness and the shining radiance are the unconditioned essence of mind. Oblivious to your delusion, you accept this majestic mind as the finished product. You believe it to be Nibbāna, the transcendent emptiness of pure mind.

"But emptiness, radiance, clarity and happiness are all subtle conditions of a mind still bound by delusion. When you observe the emptiness carefully, with sustained attention, you will observe that it is not really uniform, not really constant. The emptiness produced by primal delusion is the result of subtle conditions. Sometimes it changes a little — just a little — but enough for you to know that it's transient. Subtle variations can be detected, because all conditioned phenomena — no matter how refined, bright and majestic they seem — invariably manifest some irregular symptoms.

"If it is truly Nibbāna, why does this refined state of the mind display a variety of subtle conditions? It is not constant and true. Focus on that luminous center to see clearly that its radiance has the same characteristics — of being transient, imperfect and unessential — as all the other phenomena that you have already transcended. The only difference is that the radiance is far more subtle and refined.

"Try imagining yourself standing in an empty room. You look around and see only empty space — everywhere. Absolutely nothing occupies that space — except you, standing in the middle of the room. Admiring its emptiness, you forget about yourself. You forget that you occupy a central position in that space. How then can the room be empty? As long as someone remains in the room, it is not truly empty. When you finally realize that the room can never be truly empty until you depart, that is the moment when that fundamental delusion about your true self disintegrates, and the pure, delusion-free mind arises.

"Once the mind has let go of phenomena of every sort, the mind appears supremely empty; but the one who admires the emptiness, who is awestruck by the emptiness, that one still survives. The self as reference point, which is the essence of all false knowing, remains integrated into the mind's knowing essence. This self-perspective is the primary delusion. Its presence represents the difference between the subtle emptiness of the radiant mind and the transcendent emptiness of the pure mind, free of all forms of delusion. Self is the real impediment. As soon as it disintegrates and disappears, no more impediments remain. Transcendent emptiness appears. As in the case of a person in an empty room, we can say that the mind is truly empty only when the self leaves for good. This transcendent emptiness is a total and permanent disengagement that requires no further effort to maintain.

"Delusion is an intrinsically blind awareness, masquerading as radiance, clarity and happiness. As such, it is the self's ultimate safe haven. But those treasured qualities are all products of subtle causes and conditions. True emptiness occurs only when every single trace of one's conditioned reality disappears.

"As soon as you turn around and know it for what it is, that false awareness simply disintegrates. Clouding your vision with its splendor, that luminous deception has all along been concealing the mind's true, natural wonder."

Returning to the nunnery that evening, Mae Chee Kaew reflected on how the radiant mind had become her sole lingering attachment. Cherishing and safeguarding it more than anything else, she hardly wanted to interfere with it. Within the entire mind and body, nothing stood out so prominently as that luminance. It provoked such a riveting sense of inner amazement — and consequently, such a protective feeling of attachment — that she wanted nothing to disturb it.

Because of Mae Chee Kaew's delusion about the mind essence that knows all things, she forgot to investigate and pass judgment on the true nature of that essence. When the scope of the mind drew inward, it gathered itself into a radiant nucleus — bright, cheerful and bold. Every mental act arose from that nucleus. Consciousness flowed from that nucleus. Thoughts formed there. All happiness seemed to gather there. So she had believed that it must be Nibbāna, the center of her being that was so bright and clear all the time. But she now realized that it was actually the nucleus of the origin of suffering.

Fearless and unshakable, Mae Chee Kaew began to meticulously scrutinize her mind's extraordinary radiance, looking for any signs of imperfection. The luminous mind appeared unblemished, untroubled and exceedingly pure at first. But when she looked at it more closely she began to notice that an equally refined dullness occasionally emerged to tarnish that radiant, crystal-clear essence of knowing. This irregularity caused an equally subtle form of dissatisfaction and uncertainty to slip in. The minute fluctuations that she observed revealed enough variance to make her suspicious and to encourage her to persevere. Eventually she became so absorbed in attending to those fluctuations that she lost all sense of time. She completely forgot the time of day, the time for sleep, and even, how tired she was. Without letting up, she continued for days on end, noting the slightest inconsistencies as they arose, until all certainty about the radiant awareness eroded and disappeared.

WITH THE FIRST LIGHT OF DAWN on November 1, 1952, Mae Chee Kaew sensed that her body was tired. With perfect mindfulness, she had been walking barefoot on her meditation path for hours. She decided to rest for a while before going to the kitchen to prepare food for the monks' almsround. The first clear rays of dawn were beginning to illuminate the topmost foliage of the *phayom* tree, bathing its yellow flowers in the soft glow of imminent awakening. She walked slowly to the bamboo platform under the tree, and sat perfectly still for a long moment — a moment of deep, still, unfocused calm. A prolonged lull ensued where nothing moved forward, nothing moved back and nothing stood still. Then, aware but knowing nothing in particular, suspended in emptiness, the crystal-clear radiance of mind she had treasured for so long suddenly turned and dissolved — revealing a pure, all-knowing presence that filled the heart and pervaded the entire universe. The knower was everywhere, but nothing was known. Without characteristics and without source, emanating from no point in particular, knowing was simply a spontaneous happening of cosmic expanse. The radiant awareness had dissolved in an instant, leaving only purity of mind and the essential freedom of pure Dhamma — an absolutely unconditioned knowing that entirely transcended all forms of human conception.

"Body, mind and essence are all distinct and separate realities. Absolutely everything is known — earth, water, fire and wind; body, feeling, memory, thought and consciousness; sounds, sights, smells, tastes, touches and emotions; anger, greed and delusion — all are known. I know them all as they exist — in their own natural states. But no matter how much I am exposed to them, I am unable to detect even an instant when they have any power over my heart. They arise, they cease. They are forever changing. But the presence that knows them never changes for an instant. It is forever unborn and undying. This is the end of all suffering."

Part Four
Purity

People say they want to reach Nibbana so they crane their necks and look up into the vastness of space. They don't realize that no matter how far and hard they look, they still can't find it. It simply isn't within the realm of conventional reality.

River and Ocean

Rivers flow inexorably towards the sea, each with its own name and state of being. Once emptied into the vast ocean, however, the waters merge into one essential element and the rivers lose their individual identities. The river water is still there but it no longer has separate characteristics apart from the ocean. River and ocean are neither the same, nor are they different. In a similar way, Mae Chee Kaew's pure essence of being had merged into the boundless ocean of Nibbāna. The essence was the same; it had not changed. But it was indistinguishable from Nibbāna's essential element of pure Dhamma. And just as the river water cannot reunite with the stream, so the merged essence of mind can no longer link with past moments of consciousness that give birth to the illusion of self continuity. Living in the timeless present, devoid of past and future, the essence does not reap the fruits of old *kamma* or sow the seeds of new *kamma*. It no longer leaves the slightest trace to mark its existence.

For days, the enlightened essence completely absorbed Mae Chee Kaew's attention. The radiance of mind that she had valued so highly now appeared coarse and sullied by comparison, like dung next to gold. Eventually, through the natural flow of consciousness, the mind essence began reconnecting with her faculties of awareness and with the physical presence of her body — those factors of her worldly personality that were still bound to the cycle of birth and death. Mae Chee Kaew's conscious mind and her physical body were the surviving remnants of eons of past *kamma*, and they would continue to experience the consequences of those past actions until their disintegration at the time of death. Though all attachment to them had been dissolved in the great ocean of Nibbāna, body and mind continued to function normally in their own natural spheres. But, because the mind essence was purified, each thought was an expression of freedom from delusion, and each gesture was an expression of enlightenment. Living *in* the world, but no longer *of* the world, Mae Chee Kaew's mind was untouched by mundane desires.

Because her body and mind were results of the past *kamma* that lingered on, she thought to unravel the fabric of her past existence to see where it led. Through the power of her divine eye she began to reflect upon the lack of a beginning to the history of her former embodiment. She was amazed to find out how many times she had been born and how many times she had died; to see how many lifetimes she had spent traversing the immeasurable expanse of sentient existence. If the countless corpses that she had discarded along the way were scattered across the countryside, there would not be an empty stretch of ground left. Imagine the amount of time it took to be born and to die that many times! It was impossible to count all the births and deaths. There were far, far too many to even try. She felt deep dismay as she reviewed her past. Why, being born into suffering so often, had she constantly endeavored to be born again?

Eventually her focus turned to the innumerable corpses that have been discarded at death by each and every person living in the world. She saw the same situation everywhere. All living beings, whether male or female, have exactly the same history of death and rebirth; all are caught in the same vicious cycle. Everyone is equal in that respect. There is no injustice and no inequality — just karmic causes and conditions leading to the many recurring forms of becoming and dissolution. Stretching back indefinitely, she saw sentient existence crowded with the remains of death and decay. It was an unforgettable sight.

Mae Chee Kaew had always been compassionate — she was deeply sympathetic to the spiritual fate of her fellow human beings. But the reality of the supreme Dhamma which now filled her heart transcended all forms of human conception. How could she possibly explain the true nature of that Dhamma to others? Even if she tried, ordinary people, steeped in delusion, could never hope to comprehend such extraordinary purity of mind. She was unlikely to find enough receptive ears to make teaching worthwhile. Consequently, Mae Chee Kaew initially felt little incentive to speak about her experience. As though, having found a way out, she was satisfied to escape alone. She was free to live a life of perfect solitude for her remaining years. It was sufficient that she had fully realized her lifelong aspiration of reaching Nibbāna. She saw no reason to burden herself with troublesome teaching duties.

Further reflection led her to the Lord Buddha and his guiding role in revealing the true path to the cessation of suffering. Reconsidering the transcendent Dhamma and the path she took to uncover it, she finally recognized herself in everyone else: she too was a person like them. Certainly others with strong spiritual tendencies were equally as capable as she was. Reverently reviewing all aspects of the Buddha's teaching, she saw its relevance for people the world over, and its potential rewards for those who were willing to practice correctly. Those insights gave her a renewed desire to help every living being that was willing to listen.

Mae Chee Kaew had spent nearly two years in virtual seclusion within the nunnery, striving for liberation with a single-minded intensity. Now she shed her self-isolation to become more intimately involved with the day-to-day matters of her monastic community. She wanted to ensure, as best she could, that each of her spiritual companions had the best opportunity to realize her full potential. She was, however, somewhat handicapped in her teaching skills. Mae Chee Kaew, the person, was essentially a simple, uneducated countrywoman who had never been very eloquent or articulate when expressing her ideas. Being a karmic legacy of her transient personality, this deeply-ingrained aspect of her character did not change. She was only comfortable when speaking in the local Phu Tai dialect, voicing her remarks in the plain and earthy language of rural folk. Rhetorical skill was a gift that she had never possessed. For that reason, her teachings tended to be brief, direct and simple — succinct explanations that cut straight to the heart of the matter, leaving much of the broader implications to the listener's own deduction. While Mae Chee Kaew knew intuitively the fundamental moral bias of each person's heart, and the advice that each needed to hear, she was hampered in articulating that guidance in a lengthy discourse by an inability to elaborate and expand verbally on her mind's conceptual formations. To Mae Chee Kaew's clear and penetrating wisdom, those who really knew the truth remained silent, while those who talked often about the truth, in fact, knew very little.

Life at Baan Huay Sai nunnery had maintained a balance between focus on the meditation practice and service to the local community, and Mae Chee Kaew found herself in a central position to address the needs and aspirations of both sides. Realizing that each nun was practicing at a specific level in her meditation, she encouraged her sisters individually in their practice, speaking from the unique perspective of someone who had passed through all levels, and beyond all barriers. Her uncompromising diligence made her presence an inspiration to all the nuns — a living testament to their own inherent possibilities.

Decades of enduring the rigors of village life had given her an empathetic appreciation of the burdens borne by village women in their daily lives. Now, she advised them on the smallest and most mundane matters with simple, homespun wisdom born of respect and mutual understanding. Those who entered the nunnery to seek her help encountered her serene countenance and a heartfelt joy that lifted ordinary people to a higher and brighter conscious plane beyond the suffering of their mundane existence. Most of all, she took a special interest in the welfare of invisible beings from the nonphysical planes of existence. In the late hours of the night, she often received guests from the various spirit realms. She ministered to ghosts and celestial beings in equal numbers, employing a fluency in silent dialogue that she had mastered from an early age. Because those discussions were communicated in the language of the heart, thus circumventing the constraints of verbal expression, her advice flowed freely, as unbounded as her pure love and compassion. Because of those special talents, Mae Chee Kaew felt a personal responsibility toward the inhabitants of the spirit worlds for the rest of her life. Even in old age and failing health, she never tired of lending her assistance.

From birth through childhood, we've depended on our parents and teachers as we've grown and matured. We are here today because of the help they have given us. We owe them an enormous debt of gratitude.

Unstinting Gratitude

Ajaan Mahā Boowa and his disciples remained around Baan Huay Sai village, living and practicing in the area for several more years. Through her special knowledge, Mae Chee Kaew was constantly aware of their whereabouts; their comings and goings never eluded her awareness. In 1953, after the rains retreat had finished, Ajaan Mahā Boowa witnessed a prophetic vision in his meditation. Levitating effortlessly above the ground and poised to address a large crowd of supporters, he looked down to find his ageing mother, prostrate before him. Peering mournfully into his eyes, she pleaded with him not to forget her. "Are you never going to return?" she seemed to be saying. Withdrawing from meditation, Ajaan Mahā Boowa reflected on the vision and understood it to be a clear sign that the time had come to help his mother get started on the spiritual path. Out of a deep sense of gratitude for the many sacrifices she had made on his behalf, he decided to return to his home village and ordain his 60-

year-old mother as a white-robed nun. He wished to give her the best possible opportunity for spiritual development during her remaining years. Quickly, he sent her a letter advising that she begin preparing for a *mae chee* ordination.

Ajaan Mahā Boowa asked Mae Chee Kaew to accompany him on his trip home. He felt certain that she would be an ideal companion and mentor for his mother — someone who could assist her in the initial steps on the path of practice. Because Ajaan Mahā Boowa's guidance had made her own transcendence possible, Mae Chee Kaew felt a great devotion to him, and an immense feeling of gratitude which she was eager to repay. So, together with two other nuns she traveled with Ajaan Mahā Boowa and his disciples on their long journey to Baan Taad village.

Ajaan Mahā Boowa's place of birth was located several hundred miles from Baan Huay Sai, in Udon Thani province. Upon arriving at Baan Taad village, they found his mother eagerly anticipating her new life. Straightaway they set about preparing for her ordination. Recognizing his mother was too old to wander with him through the forests and the mountains, Ajaan Mahā Boowa looked for a suitable place in the vicinity of Baan Taad village to establish a forest monastery. When a maternal uncle and his friends offered a 70-acre piece of forested land about one mile south of the village, Ajaan Mahā Boowa accepted. He decided to settle there and build a monastery where both monks and nuns could live in peaceful seclusion. He instructed his supporters to build a simple bamboo, grass-roof *sala* and small bamboo huts for the monks and the nuns.

Ajaan Mahā Boowa then took his mother, Mae Chee Kaew and a group of monks on a long journey to the southeastern province of

Chantaburi, a seaside region of fishermen and fruit growers. There they spent the rains retreat of 1954, encountering an unexpected problem that hastened their departure. His mother and Mae Chee Kaew soon found difficulties adjusting to the new, more humid climate and the unfamiliar food. It was quite unlike the plain country fare of the northeastern region. Shortly thereafter, Ajaan Mahā Boowa's mother fell ill with an undiagnosed ailment. By the end of the rains, her condition had worsened into a creeping paralysis that seriously inhibited her movements. Ajaan Mahā Boowa decided that he must quickly escort his mother back to the familiar soil of Baan Taad village and seek treatment for her condition there. By the time he and his party finally arrived home, there was a newly-erected *sala* and huts waiting to greet them in the forested grounds of the new monastery.

Once back at the new monastery, Mae Chee Kaew quickly went to work. She had always been sensitive to the natural healing properties inherent in wild forest plants. That knowledge gave her an exceptional grasp of traditional herbal medicines. She deftly foraged in the surrounding woodlands for indigenous roots and tubors, local plants to which the old *mae chee's* body was more likely to respond. Using these to good effect, Mae Chee Kaew began treating Ajaan Mahā Boowa's ailing mother. Carefully adjusting the proportions of the medicinal herbs to fit her patient's changing condition and symptoms, she nursed her teacher's mother with dedication.

Entrusting herself into Mae Chee Kaew's constant care and the therapeutic properties of her herbal remedies, Ajaan Mahā Boowa's mother gradually regained her health. She first recovered her normal range of movement. Then, after a long convalescence, lasting nearly three years, she finally regained the full use of her limbs.

During those first few years, living at Baan Taad forest monastery was extremely difficult. All the basic necessities of life were in short supply. Mae Chee Kaew and the other nuns made their robes from shrouds used to cover dead bodies. Their pillows were stuffed with straw that had been offered to the monks. Their sandals were cut from old tire treads. The food was mostly plain and unsavory, just enough to get them through each day. Mae Chee Kaew would later find it difficult to describe how hard it was to live at Baan Taad forest monastery during those early years.

By 1960, the outside world began to impact the forest meditation tradition in a way that forever altered the traditional landscape. Deforestation became rapid and pervasive, forcing the forest monks to modify, and eventually, curtail their wandering lifestyle. As the geographic environment changed, Baan Taad forest monastery found itself in the forefront of efforts to establish permanent monastic communities where practicing monks and nuns could carry on Ajaan Mun's legacy, striving to maintain the virtues of renunciation, strict discipline and intensive meditation. With his charismatic presence and forthright nature, Ajaan Mahā Boowa became a pivotal figure in efforts to maintain continuity within the fraternity of forest monks, and so preserve Ajaan Mun's unique style of practice for future generations. Displaying impeccable wisdom and great rhetorical skill, he worked tirelessly to present Ajaan Mun's life and teachings to an increasingly wider audience. Practitioners soon began gravitating to Ajaan Mahā Boowa's monastery in hopes of receiving instruction from a genuine master. The influx of seekers eventually transformed the monastery into a renowned center of Buddhist practice. In this process, Mae Chee Kaew, with her simple and unsophisticated style of speaking, remained in the shadow of her distinguished teacher, quietly advising and encouraging the women who came to join the community of monastics.

As the health of Ajaan Mahā Boowa's mother improved, Mae Chee Kaew gently persuaded her to focus fully on meditation. Wanting her to develop a solid foundation in the practice, she impressed the older woman to strive diligently and to wait patiently for the results. The pace of her progress would depend largely on the store of virtuous tendencies she had accumulated from the past, and on the amount of effort that she currently put into sitting and walking meditation. By constantly cultivating virtue and never permitting evil to enter her thoughts, her presence of mind would become clearer and her understanding more penetrating. Eventually she would realize that everything is created by the mind. The eyes see images; the ears hear sounds; the nose smells aromas; the tongue tastes flavors; the body feels sensations; and the heart experiences emotions. But the mind is aware of all those things. It knows them and thinks about them, imagining them to be something concrete and real. By cultivating spontaneous mindfulness and wisdom, the mind's activities can be seen for what they truly are: transient, unsubstantial and bound up with suffering.

Without the proper focus, defilements will drag the mind along in their wake, overwhelming it with their powerful natural momentum. Before one realizes what has happened, lust, anger, greed and delusion have taken over, and presence of mind is lost. To prevent that lapse, Mae Chee Kaew urged the elderly woman to observe her mind carefully and to learn to discern the movement of its defiling influences.

Mae Chee Kaew's words of wisdom and encouragement inspired Ajaan Mahā Boowa's mother, and put her meditation firmly on the right track. As the years past, her heart developed a solid spiritual foundation. By the time Mae Chee Kaew departed from Baan Taad forest monastery in 1967, she had succeeded in placing the elderly *mae chee* squarely on the Buddha's noble path.

Before asking a question, look for the answer
within yourself. If you search, often you will find
the answer on your own.

Lifelong Commitment

By 1967 Ajaan Mahā Boowa's mother and the other *mae chees*,
practicing under Mae Chee Kaew's guidance, were firmly established
in the principles of meditation. With Ajaan Mahā Boowa's approval,
Mae Chee Kaew respectfully took leave of him and returned to the
nunnery at Baan Huay Sai. During her long stay at Baan Taad forest
monastery, Mae Chee Kaew had worried about her sisters there and
kept in contact with them. She traveled several times a year to visit
with the nuns at Baan Huay Sai, bringing much needed supplies to
supplement their stock of basic requisites. Now, with Ajaan Mahā
Boowa's blessing, she moved back to take up residence at the nunnery she founded. Mae Chee Kaew continued to live there until she
passed away 24 years later.

In moving back to Baan Huay Sai, Mae Chee Kaew resumed her
duties as the spiritual head of the nunnery. Life there had remained
quiet and simple, with an emphasis on developing mindfulness in

every daily activity. All the nuns adhered to the strict guiding principles that Mae Chee Kaew laid down for them and conscientiously
observed the eight moral precepts. In her quiet yet forceful way, she
impressed upon everyone the virtues of renunciation:

> "Now that you have ordained and come to live in this nunnery
> with me and the other nuns, you must always think, speak
> and act with the noblest intentions. You have renounced the
> mundane world for the purpose of training yourself in the
> art of cleansing your heart. Don't concern yourself with the
> worldly life you have left behind. It's time to cease worrying
> about home and family."

She admonished the nuns never to talk about indecent matters; but
instead, to talk only about matters of real substance. She wanted them
to be exemplary monastics who were patient in their endurance of
hardship, diligent in their practice of meditation, and always striving
to learn the truth about themselves. They were not to fret about lost
opportunities of the past or anticipate future rewards. Such thoughts
would only deceive them. She warned them to fight against tendencies
to laziness, and not simply surrender to their pillows. They were to
watch their thoughts carefully and search only for the truth that lay
within their own hearts.

She wanted her students to trust the way of the Lord Buddha. At
the same time, she encouraged them to focus intently on each forward
step as they sought to find their own path. Because that path lies
within the hearts and minds of each individual, it was up to each of
her students to search within herself to discover the way to transcend

suffering. She encouraged them to remain tough-minded and diligent until they reached the final goal.

Each time that she sensed the nuns slacking, she challenged them to evaluate their progress:

"Many of you have been studying with me for a long time, but how many real successes can you count? Your present attachments far outnumber your accomplishments. If you don't believe me, ask yourself: How many attachments have I actually cut off? Even the celestial *devas* are born only to die and be born again. Just like you, they are attached to the importance of their fleeting lives. It's just this longing for birth, this longing for life, which causes all beings to be continually reborn in the world of suffering.

"There is no room for negligence in the spiritual life. You are now striving for moral virtue and true happiness. Many of us, both old and young, are living this life together. We must all patiently endure the inevitable hardships of a nun's simple existence without becoming lazy or disgruntled. Let love and compassion be your ready response to every situation. Be gentle and deferential to your spiritual sisters, and accept criticism from your teacher gratefully. When I complain about your behavior, understand that I am teaching you. My criticisms are voiced for your own good. It is imperative that you show respect to your teacher and all your fellow nuns. A junior nun is expected to bow to her seniors, even if that nun is senior merely by a single day. As long as you cheerfully accept your proper status in the community, we will all live together in a spirit of contentment. Love, compassion and sympathetic joy will develop and expand until they fill our hearts, spreading out to each other and to all living beings everywhere."

Ajaan Mahā Boowa made regular visits to the nunnery, and often lauded Mae Chee Kaew as an outstanding example for nuns and lay devotees to emulate. In truth, her practice of Dhamma was a model which all Buddhists should follow. He invited her disciples to reflect on her exceptional courage and resolve, and on her supreme wisdom and compassion. They were the qualities that buoyed her practice and steadied her course, and finally delivered her to the deathless state beyond all possibility of deterioration. Transcending both suffering and happiness, Mae Chee Kaew practiced the Dhamma teaching of the Fully Enlightened One, the Lord Buddha, to its ultimate transcendence.

As disciples of the Buddha, we mustn't live our lives only to rot and decompose without having found anything genuine within ourselves. When death comes, die letting go of the body and the mind, laying them down without attachment.

Pureness of Heart

For the next ten years Mae Chee Kaew energetically committed herself to the spiritual well-being of the community she had founded. Then, suddenly, in June of 1977 she fell seriously ill. The symptoms had been accumulating in her body for some time. But, not wanting to inconvenience others, she had kept quiet about them. When her condition became too obvious to hide, she was admitted to a hospital. The doctors discovered that she had tuberculosis in one of her lungs. Further tests revealed that she had diabetes as well. By then her body was weak and pale, and racked by severe pain. Her symptoms had already reached a critical stage. Fearful of the worst, the medical staff suspected that her case was terminal. The most favorable prognosis was that she might live another year or two with constant medical attention. Then, when Mae Chee Kaew started wheezing and coughing blood, more tests were administered. The doctors discovered a malignant tumor lodged within her other lung.

With three diseases now confirmed — tuberculosis, diabetes and cancer — her prospects for survival dimmed.

A month after being admitted, Mae Chee Kaew insisted on leaving the hospital and returning to her nunnery, even though her condition remained very critical. If she was going to die, she preferred to die in the peace and tranquility of the forest she loved, surrounded by the care and affection of her spiritual companions. Although her body was weighed down by sickness, her heart was free of all burdens. Mae Chee Kaew was not concerned for her own well-being, and she had no fear of dying. The welfare of her companions, her supporters and her friends was far more important to her. Her nature shone with a clear brightness that illuminated their paths and lightened their hearts. Difficulties seemed to dissolve in the presence of her pure love. There was only one place she wanted to live out her final days: the place where she could be of the greatest benefit to the most people.

A medical doctor from Bangkok, a lady devotee named Dr. Pensri Makaranon, volunteered to join Mae Chee Kaew at Baan Huay Sai to oversee her medical treatment. Dr. Pensri, who had been a practicing physician for 20 years, started by treating the tuberculosis and the diabetes with the most up-to-date remedies known to her profession. She administered a strict regimen of antibiotics to counter the tuberculosis and gave regular insulin injections to curb the diabetes. But, for the cancer, she had no remedy; so administered none.

Dr. Pensri would later recall that treating Mae Chee Kaew was the hardest assignment of her medical career. She felt she lacked the spiritual training needed to treat an arahant to the best of her ability, while at the same time not being disrespectful of the wishes of her enlightened patient. Aware that people who recover from one disease are bound to die from another, Dr. Pensri focused on treating the sick person rather than the disease. Since Mae Chee Kaew was certain to die one day anyway, the doctor simply tried her best to ensure Mae Chee Kaew remained as comfortable as possible. For this reason, every time that Dr. Pensri wanted to give Mae Chee Kaew a particular medicine, the doctor would describe her diagnosis and explain the recommended treatment. It was then up to Mae Chee Kaew whether to accept or not. If she refused, Dr. Pensri would not pressure her in any way.

Though it dragged on for another 14 years, ill health did not prevent Mae Chee Kaew from fulfilling her religious obligations and practicing meditation. She simply continued to live life as best she could, compensating for infirmity by adapting her daily routine to fit the increasing limitations imposed by physical decline. Her presence exuded an exceptional gentleness and humility. She never tired of extolling the virtues of those who gave her assistance. In appreciation of the doctor's generosity, she always held the medicines she received above her head with both hands before taking them. She met each person who came to her nunnery in the same way, without bias, and responded to their queries with inspirational words of wisdom. Her mind remained clear, and she kept teaching. Knowing that the human body is caught in a relentless march toward death, she accepted her condition without regrets, and selflessly shared her remaining time and energy with those who came to seek her grace.

Throughout her prolonged infirmity, Mae Chee Kaew found eating and digesting food increasingly more difficult. As a consequence, she ate only sparingly, one tiny mouthful at a time. Most of her teeth were lost to the ravages of old age, so she chewed very slowly and deliberately, often taking an hour to finish a meager portion of food. Sometimes, due to weakness or disinterest, she nodded off while chewing. She knew the human form to be devoid of lasting essence; but bearing it was, nonetheless, truly a heavy burden. And the older and frailer she grew, the more of a drag that weight became.

Mae Chee Kaew's physical frame crumbled bit by bit; her faculties slowly wasted away. Knowing the truth of human embodiment, she expected no less. She became afflicted with glaucoma in one eye, which caused her blood pressure to rise dangerously. But she staunchly refused to seek medical treatment. Nature was simply taking its course, so let it be. Many months later, when an examination was finally arranged, the doctors discovered that the glaucoma had caused her to go blind in one eye. The other eye was overlaid by a cloudy film of cataract, though its effect was not so severe as to prevent her from seeing.

She also suffered from a debilitating backache, which caused her to walk in a stoop that greatly impaired her movements. Her legs became weak, and soon she was unable to move around without help. Eventually, she woke up one morning to find that she could no longer walk. She must now be carried everywhere, even for bathing and relieving herself.

Mae Chee Kaew had dedicated her life to Buddhism in a spirit of love and friendship. Even as death approached, she set an example of working tirelessly to help others, leaving a lasting impression on her close disciples and on the doctor who nursed her so devotedly. Even though her body was tormented with pain, she remained unperturbed and never complained. Free from suffering, knowing the many realms of sentient existence, knowing her past births and her present enlightenment, knowing how to perform miracles and read the minds of others, Mae Chee Kaew was serenely unmoved by the strains of physical hardship.

Chin sagging, face sunken, skin ashen and deeply wrinkled, Mae Chee Kaew's body lay on its deathbed, proclaiming loudly the unmistakable signs of age and sickness. Its life-sustaining faculties were slowly succumbing to the strain, wearing down and ebbing away, as though the life force was preparing to vacate. Body and mind waited for past *kamma* to release its grip, and allow their breakup to commence. But, empty of both mind and body, the indestructible pure essence pervaded everything, and awaited nothing.

When Ajaan Mahā Boowa came to visit his ailing disciple that day, he advised her medical attendants to allow nature to take its course. Mae Chee Kaew had lived her life for the sake of others. It was time now for them to let her die in peace. They should not disturb an arahant's final passing away. By that time, her lungs had become so dense and clogged with fluid that she could scarcely take a breath. Her emaciated body lay stiff and motionless, her mouth sagging open, her eyes half closing. Listening for signs of life, her attendants could no longer hear the sounds of breathing. It was obvious that the end was nearing, and none of them dared to take their eyes off her. As her breathing grew fainter and finer, tapering off ever so gently, it finally appeared to cease altogether. It ended so delicately, so serenely, that no one was sure at which precise moment she had finally passed away. Her physical presence remained so still and tranquil that it revealed nothing out of the ordinary.

Mae Chee Kaew passed away in perfect peace on the morning of June 18, 1991. Her individual essence, flowing freely like a stream, merging with rivers and seas, had at last dissolved completely into a vast, still ocean of timeless emptiness. Soon afterward, Ajaan Mahā Boowa came to view her body. He stood silently for a long while contemplating the withered corpse wrapped neatly in a fine white cloth, then solemnly performed a ritual bathing. He set June 23 as the date for her cremation, which allowed sufficient time for her relatives and faithful followers in distant locations to pay their final respects and participate in the ceremony. Ajaan Mahā Boowa refused to permit any funeral chanting during the ceremony, reasoning that since Mae Chee Kaew was already fully accomplished within herself, nothing further needed to be added.

On the evening of June 22, Ajaan Mahā Boowa delivered a Dhamma oration to inspire the large crowd of monks and supporters who had gathered to honor Mae Chee Kaew, the foremost female arahant of the modern era.

> "In death, Mae Chee Kaew directs our attention to the true nature of this world: for all of us, without exception, will die one day. Being born as human beings, we should make good use of this auspicious birth, as it is our best opportunity to strive for spiritual perfection within our hearts. There is no reason to doubt the Lord Buddha's teaching. The Four Noble Truths stand as testimony to its veracity. If we faithfully follow the Buddha's teaching in our meditation practice, we will inevitably develop the paths and their fruition to perfection.
>
> "As long as there are people who practice Buddhism properly, the world will never be devoid of arahants. Mae Chee Kaew was a shining example of this truth, a present-day arahant of rare virtue. She died, just like the rest of us will; however, it

was the virtuous qualities she developed deep within her heart that are the real significance — the true essence of her being — and not her death. The heart is fundamental. It dictates all of our actions, both good and bad. So it is incumbent on us to develop our hearts to the fullest while we still have the opportunity to do so."

Mae Chee Kaew's cremation ceremony took place on the following afternoon, inside the nunnery compound at Baan Huay Sai. More than 200 monks and thousands of devoted lay followers were in attendance to pay their final homage. In a gesture of devotion and respect, long lines of monks, nuns and lay devotees filed past her casket, placing bright blossoms made from fragrant sandalwood shavings around the ornate casket, until they were heaped high on the funeral pyre. As the crowd sat in reverent silence, Ajaan Mahā Boowa touched a flame to the dry tinder beneath the casket. Flames shot up and palls of thick smoke billowed around the pyre and into the hot afternoon air. Suddenly, and quite unexpectedly, a cooling, gentle rain began to fall on the entire assembly.

Late that evening, when the fire had burned itself out and the ashes began to crumble and cool, monks and nuns gathered silently around the smoldering remains of Mae Chee Kaew's funeral pyre. The extreme heat of the pyre had caused the bones in her body to break apart and disintegrate, leaving behind many small porous fragments bleached to an ashen-white hue by the fire. Gingerly, with a sense of awe and reverence, senior monks picked bone fragments from the gray ash and charcoal, placing the pieces carefully on trays of white cloth. The relics were retrieved with great care and kept solemnly until the following morning, when countless bone fragments from Mae Chee Kaew's body were shared among her faithful supporters as sacred keepsakes. They have been cherished ever since as rare gems of unblemished virtue. Being the relics of an arahant, they are infused with a supramundane, spiritual potency that blesses those who possess them with good fortune — and even seeming miracles — in direct proportion to the strength of faith and virtue that the owners maintain in their hearts.

In the following months and years, many of those pieces of bone underwent a miraculous transformation. Over time, the physical elements gradually coalesced and crystallized, forming dense, hard gemstones — some translucent and angular like crystal, others colorful and polished smooth like beach pebbles. Such bone relics, the physical remnants of an arahant's pure essence, are an ineffable mystery of the mind's pure essence: lifeless bone fragments transmuting into diamonds and pearls. They indicate the cleansing effect that the pure mind of the arahant exerts on the body's material elements. The intrinsic level of samādhi that an arahant maintains throughout all daily activities works steadily to cleanse those basic elements until they too become purified. That purifying action results in a transmutation of ordinary bone into crystalline relics after they pass away. The extraordinary beauty and brilliance of Mae Chee Kaew's bone relics were often cited as proof — should further proof be needed — that she was indeed an *ariya sāvikā*, a genuine daughter of the Lord Buddha.

Epilogue

Ajaan Inthawai Santussako, a highly-respected senior monk in the Thai forest tradition, took a special interest in Mae Chee Kaew and her enduring legacy. Born in a village near Baan Huay Sai, and ordained as a novice monk at the age of eleven, he had known Mae Chee Kaew since childhood. It was reputed that they shared a spiritual connection spanning many lifetimes — a karmic relationship Mae Chee Kaew herself frequently acknowledged. Shortly after the funeral, Ajaan Inthawai resolved to honor her memory with a monument giving form and vision to her simple grace and pure compassion. He envisioned a place where people from all walks of life could gather to recollect her extraordinary virtue and pay homage to the relics of a female arahant.

After many years of careful planning, his vision finally became a reality. Together with a group of railway engineers from Bangkok, Ajaan Inthawai designed and built a memorial stupa with a broad trapezoidal base topped by a gracefully tapering spire. The building took shape on a high, flat stretch of ground adjacent to Baan Huay Sai nunnery — an imposing structure that rises nearly 80 feet from the base to the crown. The stupa housing her relics is surrounded by a circular pool of cool clear water, its surface bursting with pink and purple lotus blossoms. The water is rimmed by landscaped sections of tropical flower gardens interspersed with natural rock formations and hedged by rows of neatly trimmed shrubbery. Tall, shady trees line the outer periphery. An atmosphere of unusual peace and serenity pervades the entire area.

The Mae Chee Kaew Memorial Stupa was officially opened on May 21, 2006. It has since become a place of pilgrimage for devout Buddhists from all over the world. Her magnificent relics, with their gemstone-like qualities, are prominently displayed on the altar. The stupa is home to three life-size statues of Mae Chee Kaew. Tucked into the main alcove is a standing statue of Mae Chee Kaew made of composite materials. On the second floor of the stupa, high on the shrine's altar sits an elegant wax reproduction, dressed in the white robes of a *mae chee*. A pure-white fiberglass statue of her walking in meditation dominates the stupa's ground floor. The intricately-crafted copper doors and windows on the second floor were designed and built by a renowned national artist.

Ajaan Mahā Boowa kindly presided over the official opening ceremony, when her relics were formally enshrined in the stupa.

"On this auspicious occasion we are honoring Mae Chee Kaew, a noble disciple of Ajaan Mun whose bones have now been transformed into exquisite crystal relics. The attainment of arahantship is not based on gender. When any person, whether male or female, succeeds in eliminating all mental defilements through the perfection of spiritual virtue, that person becomes an arahant. All of us should strive to follow the superb example Mae Chee Kaew set by perfecting spiritual virtue within our own hearts. A wholehearted respect for her supreme spiritual achievement is equivalent to worshipping the Lord Buddha, the Dhamma and the Sangha. We can all take refuge in her unblemished purity."

Collected Teachings

Being born into this world, you must rely on your innate wisdom. You can seek pain or pleasure, seek things of value or things of no value at all. Depending on the direction you choose, you can find heaven or hell, or the paths and fruitions leading to Nibbāna. You can find anything: it's up to you to decide.

The goodness of others is their own. We cannot share the fruits of their actions, so we must do good deeds ourselves.

Do not doubt the efficacy of *kamma* or underestimate the consequences of your actions. As human beings, we should feel compassion for the suffering of all living beings, because we all experience suffering as a result of our past deeds. In this regard, everyone is equal. What differentiates us as good or bad, coarse or refined, is the kind of actions that we have done in the past.

You can't grow enough grass by yourself to thatch every roof in town. Be generous within your means.

Don't go around boasting and bragging to the whole town. If something makes you look bad, you'll have to go hide, like a frog that jumps down into the water as soon as it sees someone coming. If you're dumb, don't advertise yourself as clever.

Those who fail to restrain their speech are unaware of whether they are right or wrong in what they say. Those who know the truth usually remain silent; those who often talk of truth know very little about it.

Be determined to keep watch over your bodily actions, speech and mind, and conduct yourself with composure. Don't talk too much or create difficulties for yourself. Don't lose your self-control or be disrespectful to your elders. Watch your words, and laugh with restraint.

No matter how close you are with someone, don't let your speech become careless. No matter how frustrated you are, don't let your speech become angry.

Don't be crafty and sly, trying to fool people into thinking you're a good person when you're not. Someone who feigns virtue and intelligence is actually a dumb, silly fool who lacks moral goodness.

Having been born into the world, we attach importance to the days and the months and the years as they pass. We believe in the importance of our lives and the lives of others. For this reason, our minds are constantly concerned with pain and suffering. No sooner do we take birth than we cling on tightly to our precarious state and start to worry. We are afraid of this and fear that. Our minds are immediately consumed by worldly influences and deluded tendencies driven by greed, hatred and fear. We are born with this condition, and if we don't do something about it now, we will die still carrying those tendencies with us. What a shame!

Suffering — once we're born, that's all we have; wanting, not wanting, being satisfied or dissatisfied; sitting, lying, eating, relieving ourselves — but there's no relief. Suffering is always there. So when we meditate, we should examine this heap of suffering in its entirety.

We are never satisfied. We like to hear the sound of birds singing, but then become annoyed when they get too noisy.

People's hearts are so clogged up with pain and suffering they cannot see anything clearly. By leaping after their desires and delighting in them, stupid people welcome suffering with open arms. They mistake suffering for happiness. Smart people look inside and examine themselves until they see what happiness truly is and what suffering truly is. Their hearts are not so easily blocked. When they see stubbornness in themselves, they recognize stubbornness. When they see gloom, they recognize gloom. When they see stupidity, they recognize that too. They look for their own faults; they don't try to fault other people.

Moral virtue is founded in renunciation. True goodness is found in the heart.

Look carefully at your own heart and mind. Examine them closely. There alone is where you'll find heaven and hell, the noble path leading to enlightenment, and that which is secure, beyond all pain and suffering.

Don't be resentful of criticism or prideful of praise. Simply stay focused on your meditation practice from dawn to dusk. Develop spiritual virtue day and night, and always speak the truth.

Self-honesty is the basis of moral virtue. Know yourself, accept your faults and work to overcome them. Hide nothing from yourself. Above all, don't lie to yourself. Lying to yourself is a fundamental breach of moral virtue. You can lie to the entire world if you like, but you must never lie to yourself.

Cultivate your mind, as a farmer cultivates his fields. Gradually clear the land; prepare the soil; plough the rows; sow the seeds; spread the manure; water the plants and pull the weeds and, eventually, you will reap a golden harvest.

If you don't practice, you won't learn how to meditate. If you don't see the truth for yourself, you won't really understand its meaning.

Don't remain idle, claiming that you're too cold in the morning, too hot in the afternoon and too sleepy in the evening, and then complain you don't have time to practice meditation. Don't listen to the defiling tune of laziness and oppose the teaching of the wise. A timid person who listens only to himself is so busy groping for his pillow he can never make progress along the path to enlightenment.

Be determined to develop your mind by diligently practicing meditation. Dedicate your body and mind to the search for Dhamma. Use your heart as a torch to light the way. Be resolute on the path, and you will transcend suffering. As a human being, you should strive to be virtuous and never belittle the importance of Dhamma.

Maintain moral virtue and meditate with diligence. It doesn't cost you a penny. Avoid being lazy. When calm and insight are fully developed, the mind will be far removed from defilement. Give up all attachments and transcend the world of suffering. The result is Nibbāna.

Hurry up and establish a secure refuge within yourself. If you don't, when you die, your heart will have no firm basis to fall back on. Every living being without exception experiences birth and death. Each person who is born must die and be reborn again and again in a continuous cycle of suffering and hardship. People of every age group and social status are equal in this respect. Perhaps we'll die in the morning, perhaps in the evening, we don't know. But we can be certain that death will come when the time is ripe.

We are born and we die again and again. Birth, aging and death cycle on. Being descendents of the Lord Buddha, we mustn't live our lives only to rot and decompose without having found anything genuine within ourselves. When death comes, die properly, die with purity. Die letting go of the body and mind, laying them down without attachment. Die in touch with the true nature of things. Die following the footsteps of the Lord Buddha. Die thus, and become "deathless."

Listen to me! Don't just eat and sleep like a common animal. Make sure you remain disenchanted with worldly life and have a healthy fear of all future birth. Open your heart to true happiness. Don't just sit around idly, keeping vigil over the smoldering embers of your life.

Knowledge about the world we live in may be useful, but no other knowledge compares with truly knowing yourself. The understanding arising through our physical eye is very different from that of our inner spiritual eye. The superficial understanding that we gain from thought and reflection is not the same as deep understanding born of insight into something's true nature.

Someone once asked Ajaan Mun: "What books do forest meditation monks study?" His reply was: "They study with eyes closed, but mind awake." As soon as I awaken in the morning, my eyes are bombarded by forms; so, I investigate the contact between eye and form. My ears are struck by sounds, my nose by aromas, and my tongue by flavors; my body senses hot and cold, hard and soft, while my heart is assailed by thoughts and emotions. I investigate all these things constantly. In that way, each of my sense faculties becomes a teacher; and I am learning Dhamma the whole day without a break. It's up to me which sense faculty I choose to focus on. As soon as I'm focused, I try to penetrate to the truth of it. That's how Ajaan Mun taught me to meditate.

The body is an important object of craving; and the resulting attachment is a tenacious defilement. Suffering is the consequence. To overcome it, focus your attention on the decay and disintegration of the human body so that the mind becomes clearly disgusted with the human condition, thoroughly weary of the true nature of human embodiment. As repulsion to the physical grows stronger, lightness and brightness of mind become more prominent. The human body is a heap of flesh and blood two feet wide and six feet long that is changing every moment. Seeing the suffering caused by our attachment to the body, is the initial insight that focuses our minds on Dhamma. Those who see the body clearly tend to understand Dhamma quickly.

When strange and unusual things occur in your meditation, just let them happen. Don't become attached to them. Such things are really an external focus and should be let go of. Put them down and move on — don't hold on to them. All realms of consciousness originate from the mind. Heaven and hell originate from the mind. *Pretas* and *devas,* lay people, nuns — all living beings originate from the mind. Because of that, it is far better to focus exclusively on your own mind. There you will find the whole universe.

In a perfectly still, crystal-clear pool of water, we can see everything with clarity. The heart at complete rest is still. When the heart is still, wisdom appears easily, fluently. When wisdom flows, clear understanding follows. The world's impermanent, unsatisfactory and insubstantial nature is seen in a flash of insight, and we become fed up with our attachment to this mass of suffering and loosen our grip. In that moment of coolness, the fires in our heart abate, while freedom from suffering arises naturally of its own accord. This transformation occurs because the original mind is, by its very nature, absolutely pure and unblemished. Purity is its normal state. It becomes blemished only because it accepts external intrusions, which themselves cause emotions like sadness and joy to arise and proliferate until the mind becomes totally blinded to its own true nature. In the end, it is inundated with the murky waters of the world, swimming crazily in its own pool of craving.

Everything is created by our minds. The eyes see images, the ears hear sounds, the nose smells aromas, the tongue tastes flavors, the body feels sensations, and the heart experiences emotions. But the mind is aware of all these things. It knows them and it thinks about them, imagining them to be this or that. When our mindfulness and wisdom are strong, we can see these creations for ourselves. But mostly the defilements carry us along in their flow, in their powerful natural momentum. Before we realize what has happened, we become angry, greedy, deluded or conceited — because we've been deceived by the defilements. So please watch the ebb and flow of those defiling influences carefully. Don't let them deceive you so readily. When we are skilled enough to keep up with their movements, we can transform their negative power into positive spiritual energy.

Strive diligently and be patient. The pace of your progress depends largely on the store of virtuous tendencies you have accumulated from the past, and on the amount of present-moment effort you put into sitting and walking meditation. So always cultivate virtue and never let evil thoughts enter your mind. The more you practice in this way, the clearer your presence of mind will become, and the more comprehensive your understanding will be. As knowledge concerning your own true nature blossoms and blooms within your heart, the end of the long road of suffering will gradually come into view.

But if you neglect to cultivate your inherent mindfulness and wisdom, striving halfheartedly, indifferent to the truth about yourself, the obstacles in your path will grow and multiply until they block all sight of the way, leaving the end of the road forever in darkness.

People say they want to go to Nibbāna so they crane their necks and look up into the vastness of space. They don't realize that no matter how far and hard look, they still can't find Nibbāna. It simply isn't within the realm of conventional reality.

The practices that I have maintained all these years are not easy to do — they are extremely difficult. I have endured many hardships to test my determination and my stamina along the path. I have gone without food for many days. I have refused to lie down to sleep for many nights. Endurance became the food to nourish my heart and diligence became the pillow to rest my head. Try it for yourself. Test your resolve. You will soon discover the mysterious power of your own mind.

Be a nun in the truest sense. You don't want to spoil your vocation by mingling with the foul-smelling grit of worldly life, so don't glance back, longing for your home and family. Avoid being a lazy nun who talks a lot and asks for favors. Always be satisfied with living a simple life, and never be afraid of death. Never talk about indecent matters; instead, talk about matters of real substance. My nuns should always behave properly. If you truly wish to be my disciples, pay attention to what I say. When I complain about your behavior, understand that I am teaching you to always follow my example in whatever you do.

You who have come here to be my students, make the effort to become exemplary human beings. Be beautiful nuns who are patient in your endurance of hardship and diligent in your practice of meditation, always striving to learn the truth about yourselves.

My students should trust the way of the Lord Buddha, focusing intently on each forward step. Don't fret about lost opportunities of the past or anticipate future rewards. Such thoughts will only deceive you. Fight against any tendencies to laziness — don't simply surrender to your pillow. Watch your mind carefully and search for the truth within your own heart.

Before asking a question, look for the answer within yourself. If you search, often you will find the answer on your own.

In the practice of Buddhism, you must find your own path. It is up to you to search for and discover the way to transcend suffering. The correct way to search is to look inside yourself. The path lies within the hearts and minds of each of us. So be tough and remain diligent until you reach the final destination.

People suffer because they grasp and don't let go. They harbor evil intentions and ill will, and won't let go. Suffering follows them everywhere. So you must examine yourself and learn how to let go.

Don't doubt the value of meditation practice. Don't underestimate your abilities. Be content with whatever progress you make because it represents part of the truth of who you are. As such, it is something you can rely on. Consider who you really are: Who is it that is born, gets sick, grows old and dies? Your body, your mind, your life — these don't belong to you. Don't soil your true nature with the sufferings of the world.

Since the day I ordained as a nun, I have never quit cleansing my heart of impurities. I am constantly aware that I need to polish and refine my basic nature.

Only the true sage can take refuge in the cool shade of the three Bodhi trees of Buddha, Dhamma and Sangha.

About the Author

Bhikkhu Sīlaratano was born Richard E. Byrd, Jr. at Winchester, Virginia in 1948. He began his life as a Buddhist monk in 1975 in Bangalore, India where he ordained as a novice monk with Ven. Buddharakkhita Thera. While still a novice he moved to Sri Lanka, taking full bhikkhu ordination at Sri Vajiragnana Dharmayatanaya in Maharagama in June of 1976. In early 1977 Bhikkhu Sīlaratano traveled to Thailand, where he was ordained into the Dhammayutha Nikāya at Wat Bovornives Vihāra in Bangkok on April 21, 1977. He soon moved to Baan Taad Forest Monastery in Udon Thani province, where he has been living and practicing under the tutelage of Ven. Ajaan Mahā Boowa Ñāṇasampanno and his senior disciples ever since. Bhikkhu Sīlaratano's other books include *Ācariya Mun Bhūridatta Thera: A Spiritual Biography* and *Arahattamagga Arahattaphala: The Path to Arahantship*.

Other Forest Dhamma Books Publications:

Venerable Ācariya Mun Bhūridatta Thera — *A Spiritual Biography*

Paṭipadā — *Venerable Ācariya Mun's Path of Practice*

Arahattamagga Arahattaphala — *The Path to Arahantship*

Venerable Ajaan Khao Anālayo — *A True Spiritual Warrior*

Wisdom Develops Samādhi — *A Guide to the Buddha's Meditation Methods*

A Life of Inner Quality — *A Comprehensive Guide to Buddhist Practice*

Forest Dhamma — *A Selection of Talks on Buddhist Practice*

The Dhamma Teaching of Ācariya Mahā Boowa in London

Amata Dhamma — *Six Talks on Dhamma*

Things As They Are — *A Collection of Talks on Training the Mind*

Straight from the Heart — *Talks on the Practice of Meditation*

For free downloads, please visit us at:
www.ForestDhammaBooks.com

Contact us at:
fdbooks@hotmail.com
fdbooks@gmail.com